FACE
AN

FACING ANXIETY AND STRESS

Michael Lawson

HODDER AND STOUGHTON
LONDON SYDNEY AUCKLAND TORONTO

Bible quotations are taken
from the New International Version

British Library Cataloguing in Publication Data

Lawson, Michael
  Facing anxiety and stress.
  1. Anxiety—Religious aspects—Christianity
  I. Title
  248.8'6   BV4908.5

  ISBN 0-340-37215-X

Hodder and Stoughton Editorial Office: 47 Bedford Square, London WC1B 3DP

Contents

Foreword   7

1 LIFE UNDER PRESSURE   9

2 THE NATURE OF ANXIETY   24

3 THE SHAPE OF STRESS   38

4 WHEN THE ROADS CONVERGE:
STRESS AND ANXIETY TOGETHER   53

5 SOME FALSE PATHS   67

6 FINDING FREEDOM   80

7 KEEPING THE CAR ON THE ROAD:
EFFECTIVE SELF-MANAGEMENT   97

8 WHEN HELP IS NEEDED   116

9 POSTSCRIPT: IS IT POSSIBLE TO
CHANGE?   137

Foreword

As we hurtle on towards the year 2,000, it seems that
someone's foot is flat on the accelerator. This affects us in
many different ways. At any one moment we can find
ourselves trapped in the fast lane, immobilised up to the axles
on a mud verge or struggling in the exhaust of world events as
they draw us inexorably along on the highroads of this
astonishing century. In such an era it is not surprising that
anxiety and stress tend to move in beside us as passengers
when Change is riding at the wheel.

However it is not all bad news. Choose any of the world's
top hundred cities – Calcutta ... Rio ... Los Angeles ...
Nairobi ... Sydney – and we can be quite certain that within
them can be unearthed those luminous ambassadors of sanity
and peace whose influence is out of all proportion to their
numbers.

Michael Lawson, with whom I work here at All Souls
Church in London, is one of this greatly valued network that
touches every continent. To unearth him you need to search
out a residence once lived in by Charles Dickens. And here
Michael – perhaps a little bit like the former occupier – has
put his observation of people and situations to good use in
writing us a book that is full of realism, reassurance and
practical wisdom. It is based on his experience, as a Christian
pastor and counsellor, of talking to literally hundreds of
people who have sought his friendly counsel over these past
years.

As we identify with some of the cameos of life that feature
in these pages, we shall learn – and re-learn – the secrets of

knowing ourselves, of finding the resources that can help in times of stress, and of pacing ourselves for the journey, whether trapped, immobilised or struggling.

Many are the times when I have enjoyed chatting over coffee with Michael Lawson. Treat this book of his as you would a cup of friendly filter coffee, slowly and with every intent of benefiting.

I am glad that good books are still coming out of Charles Dickens' old house.

RICHARD BEWES
All Souls Church, Langham Place, London

Chapter One

LIFE UNDER PRESSURE

What is life like when we come under pressure?

Do you remember those times when you have felt worried, irritable, tense and on edge? Even perhaps so screwed up inside, that you have felt like screaming or running away? If you have experienced those kinds of feelings, or you are even going through them right now – you are not alone. So many of us, when our lives come under pressure, do feel just like this. In fact, it is almost impossible *not* to pass through some kind of stress or anxiety in life. Many people find stress and anxiety situations are an all too common, if unwelcome, part of their day-to-day experience.

So what actually are anxiety and stress, and why do they cause us so much discomfort and pain?

Is it possible to define what it is which leads to these unpleasant feelings and concerns?

In some ways it is important for us to try and do so, for if we can work out just what is going on within us, and properly define and diagnose the trouble, we shall be in a much better position to be able to cope with the situations – the stress and anxiety situations – in which we find ourselves.

Anxiety and Stress Defined

Anxiety quite clearly is to do with our fears. Any issue which crops up which in a sense provokes fear within us such as facing a totally new situation, the threat of losing a job, or coping with a difficult relationship – is potentially a cause of anxiety, because deep inside of us anxiety raises questions like: "Will I cope? Am I adequate? What will happen? Will it be all right?" It is the *fear* of what things might be like or how it may all turn out which is the dominant feeling in anxiety for most of us, and leads to our greatest sense of disease.

If anxiety is to do with our fears, then stress is perhaps more to do with our reactions to *pressure*. What kind of pressure are we talking about? It is when there is extra work to do in the office; or the children are requiring lifts home from parties, from right over the other side of town late at night; or there is increased demand to look after an elderly parent or ailing relative, on top of all your other responsibilities. All these factors provide increased pressure. After all there is only so much you can realistically be expected to do in a day!

Some people of course, seem to thrive under pressure. But actually, most of us are not too keen on it. So the way we react to those busier times of life, and the way we learn to structure our time and pace ourselves is important. Because stress is mainly to do with our *reaction* to pressure, when everything seems to hot up and make life difficult for us.

Not all in the Mind

Anxiety, then, is to do with our fears, and stress with our reaction to pressure. Of course, the two go hand in hand. Increased demands on us often bring fears and concerns as well as increasing exhaustion.

Stress and anxiety affect our bodies as well as our minds. We all find from time to time we are not coping as well as we do normally with our ordinary concerns. We become anxious about a specific situation which crops up. We have all experienced the physical symptoms produced by times like this: headache, backache, upset stomach, and many other minor ailments besides. Similarly if the pressures of our lifestyle are becoming rather too much for us: too many late nights; more tasks than time to do them; unrealistic demands from friends, family, and at work. Correspondingly we may well experience physical symptoms: disturbed sleep, irritability with those with whom we are normally calm and peaceful, indigestion, tiredness and so on.

Stress is generally more to do with the physical pressures of our lives. Anxiety more about the emotional side. But they can and do overlap. And of course there are several different factors which go to make up an anxiety or stressful situation.

To illustrate practically what life is like when we come under pressure, we will have a look at three people, Sarah, George and Jane, to see how their quite normal and everyday experiences have come about. All three are under pressure in various different ways.

When Everything Comes Together

Sarah has found a good friend in her health visitor. Since she and Peter brought baby Daniel home from the hospital three months ago, the health visitor has been very supportive. It is just as well, because in some ways it is becoming clear the family are facing particular difficulties at the moment.

Daniel is Sarah and Peter's first baby. He was a longed-for child, especially since Sarah had a miscarriage two years ago, and it was uncertain whether they would in fact be able to have children at all.

Sarah is thirty-one and Peter thirty-nine. Two months ago they both had something of a shock: Peter lost his job, very suddenly, without warning. He was working in a private bakery firm, which unfortunately had to cut its workforce rather drastically. He is still out of work, and Peter's prospects do not look too good. In this area jobs are very difficult to find. Many of those who live on the estate have been on the dole for many months, even years.

Over a cup of tea, the conversation with the health visitor covers the usual question of feeding and changing. Sarah is clearly tired, and the health visitor enquires sympathetically how she is coping generally.

"Well, I feel guilty in a way," Sarah replies. "It is such a privilege to have a baby. And Peter and I have prayed for God to give us a child for so many years. Daniel is really a wonderful baby, and we love him so much. Yet it is such a big change of routine, and I am finding it all rather draining."

"How about friends, Sarah, are you keeping in touch in any way?"

This is part of the problem. Until Daniel was on the way, Sarah was a secretary in a large, friendly office, with an excellent sports club. Those regular squash matches used to be a high spot in the week. They were invigorating. Sarah always felt they kept her physically on top.

She liked her work too. It gave her a sense of identity. The extra money helped as well. Topping up the mortgage, and setting up their new little house. And perhaps more than anything else, they were a great bunch of friends at the office. You could have a good laugh together. The contrast now is, that moving to the estate, as Sarah and Peter did seven months ago, Sarah hardly knows anyone. She misses the stimulus of her office friends. And more than that, there is Peter . . .

"Well, yes I do miss my friends. I miss them a lot. One or two have been up to see us. But we are quite difficult to get to. Public transport is appalling round here, and even finding us by car is difficult enough in the dark. They haven't even put up the names of the roads on this side of the estate yet."

"What about, Peter, is *he* being supportive?"

If Peter had not been out, Sarah would never have been able to say this. As it is, she feels bitterly disloyal, talking about him behind his back. But she has to tell someone. It is not very terrible what she is going to say, but she is very worried.

"I love Peter. Ever so much. And although it was such a blow when he lost his job, I did think it would be marvellous having him at home for a while. Especially with Daniel just arrived. I thought in some strange way it was God providing an extra support and joy for us to be together, in the midst of the sadness connected with the bakery."

"Do you mean it hasn't worked out entirely like that?"

"Yes," said Sarah. "You know Peter is very down at the moment – about losing his job and what his prospects are. It is worse than down, I think he is depressed. But he won't go and see the doctor. And when I suggested he had a talk with the vicar, he practically went through the roof."

The health visitor nodded understandingly.

"Do you feel you're propping Peter up, Sarah? You must have spent hours listening to him, if he is feeling that low."

"Oh yes, I have.´ And not just propping him up. Coping with Daniel's crying and Peter's moods as well as broken nights, and trying to keep the house clean, I'm so tired – I need support too. My mum's miles away, and even if she did come to stay, where would we put her? Besides I don't think Peter could face her coming at the moment, feeling like he is."

It was good to tell someone. And it was good also knowing that, having put her in the picture, the health visitor would be returning next week. Sarah would not have to explain it all again. Someone did understand – and cared.

When the health visitor had gone, and Sarah was thinking over what she had said to her, it became clear to Sarah that there were in fact other issues, fears really, gnawing away at her confidence. One of them came out when Peter returned from the job centre.

"There's still nothing, except washing up in that new hotel right down the centre of town. And I can't see me doing that. Honestly, Sarah, I don't know what to do." Peter looked fed up.

Sarah does not dare say it to Peter. But she is wondering how on earth they are going to manage if Peter does not get another job soon. There are so many things needing to be bought for a small baby. On their estate, they hardly know anyone who can even *lend* them things. Sarah has had faith that their needs will be met. But somehow God seems to be silent. Waiting and waiting for something to turn up is very difficult. And Sarah's confidence is waning.

But the other issue which, like the job, Sarah dare not mention to Peter, seems almost irrational, but she feels it strongly.

"I love little Daniel. I really do. But the other side of that is I feel almost totally tied to him, as though he has somehow robbed me of my freedom."

It is a kind of hemmed-in feeling. And Sarah is worried that she will lose all her friends and never be in a position to get out and make new ones. It sounds irrational to put it into words. But as Sarah put it to her health visitor when she came round the next week:

"If you ask me what I feel, I feel I'm caught in a box. I have to be the strong one around here, for the sake of Peter and Daniel. Yet in reality I feel the weakest of the lot. I'm the one who needs support. And yet I'm the one *giving it*. I feel caught. Shut in. I want to get out, and I can't."

The Pressure Mounts

George would rather be in the garden, than sitting waiting in the doctor's surgery. If it were not for these blinding headaches he has been getting recently, he would be spending his Saturday morning at home, trying to catch up with himself and the weeding. Not to mention spending a little time with Mary, his wife, and Ben and Amanda – who at fifteen and sixteen respectively, seem to be developing not only minds of their own, but also lives of their own as well.

But the real issue for George at the moment is his work. George is in his mid-forties, and works for a firm of accountants in the city. He has risen to an important position in the firm. He quite likes his colleagues, at least he can get on with them. But over these last couple of years he has grown increasingly dissatisfied with his work. When he is honest with himself, which is not always, he admits he does not care too much about what he is doing at all. It is not really him.

As George rehearses in his mind what he will say to the

doctor, his thoughts go back to last week. It could not have been worse . . .

"I suppose the thing I find so difficult is this wretched spirit of competitiveness. I mean it is not as if I don't already work all the hours God gives. I do. But some of the younger single staff don't seem to care at all if they sit there till eight o'clock in the evening, every evening. It is all very well, but some of us have families to go to."

George is right, there is certainly a pressure to work a very long concentrated day. And there is a sense you have to keep up with everyone else. But George is an old hand. He is in his third job, and he has been with this present firm for nine years. Work has always been like this. It has just been these last five weeks. What a time!

Sitting in the surgery, many issues run, even race, through George's mind.

"How am I going to explain to him what's been going on at work? It is so difficult to get over to a doctor what it *means* when one of the partners in a big city firm goes off sick. My work load has just mushroomed recently. Five weeks doing enough work for two men! I wouldn't mind if it didn't all come on my desk. But it does – no one else specialises in that area. So I have to do it. But I am beginning to feel exhausted. I'm sleeping badly, I'm getting headaches. I take only twenty minutes for lunch, queue up at the sandwich bar for ten of them, gulp down a cheese roll and a coffee, and then have to put up with indigestion for the best part of the afternoon."

The last five weeks have not been helped by the fact that George does not seem to know how to say "no". Even in his private life. Only a fortnight ago at the church where George and Mary are members, George was asked to take over as Treasurer. He does not seem to realise yet how much extra time that is going to take up. He has accepted the position, though Mary doubts she will be able to keep him in one piece, once he experiences all those extra demands on his already over-loaded timetable.

George is feeling quite low, and discouraged. It all came to a head on Thursday night.

George was waiting at Victoria Station, along with hundreds of other commuters, anxiously surveying the departures board. The train was late, fifty minutes late so far. It is so frustrating, especially when you're tired. At the best of times you can hardly ever get a seat, so there was little hope of getting an hour's sleep on the way back.

Thursday *was* a bad day. George had dictated a report last Tuesday, which came back full of typing errors. Instead of calmly correcting them, and helping the new secretary to understand the technical terms involved – he blew up at her. He did not mince his words either. She burst into tears, understandably. And it ended up with George having to apologise profusely. Realising to his shame that everybody in the office knows he is a Christian.

"So this is how Christians behave at work, eh?"

As the station's loudspeakers blandly announced yet further delays, George thought back over the last hectic few days.

"On Tuesday I had four extra meetings to go to, standing in for the partner who is away. Ben stayed out till midnight on Wednesday evening, so I didn't get to bed until twelve thirty, and then I couldn't sleep. And that girl's incompetence meant I missed lunch altogether. I feel so tired. And tense as well."

So, waiting for a train which was refusing to turn up, was not exactly balm for the wounded. When it arrived, as predicted George had to stand all the way home. Though he was very tired, he was looking forward to seeing Mary and the children soon.

But it could not have been worse. Mary had given up waiting for George at the station. There was no way of phoning her to let her know the train would be late. So George walked home in the rain, without his umbrella, and arrived cross, dishevelled, and tired – only to be greeted by the accusing-sounding unison of Ben and Amanda:

"Where have you been, Dad? You're late. We've all had supper."

That finished it. Uncharacteristically George began to bubble up with anger inside. He snapped back at Ben:

"If you knew what a day's hard work is really like, you'd have the right to speak. Since you don't know, it would be better if you kept your mouth shut."

It was so uncharacteristic, that Mary, as she came through the door realised there was something wrong. And she was right – for the first time ever that evening, George consistently snapped at Mary, arguing bitterly with the children. Of course, it did not go on for ever. By bedtime, George found himself apologising again. To the children. To Mary. He explained to them how jittery he felt, unable to relax. And he explained it all by reference to those really rotten headaches he had been getting for the past few weeks.

And that is exactly what George tells the doctor.

Feeling Unsettled

"I don't know what's come over her."

"She's never been that snappy before."

"It is so unlike her – storming off like that after a rehearsal."

It is two of Jane's friends talking. The college bar is full of students. There is so much noise, they practically have to shout above the din. Everybody seems to need to let off steam at the moment. It is getting towards the end of the summer term. Final exams are looming, the pressures are building up.

Jane's two friends peer at each other through the smoke-laden atmosphere. Sipping their drinks, trying as best they can to be heard, they continue their discussion of Jane's unexpected behaviour.

Meanwhile Jane is making her way back to her flat. A friend has offered her a lift. But Jane sits quietly and uncommunicatively in the passenger seat. Her friend, after several unsuccessful tries, decides to leave her alone and say nothing.

Jane is in her final year at college. She is twenty-one, and normally a bright outgoing person, popular with everyone. Her long blonde hair and lovely smooth complexion, together with a sharp mind and good humour, have made her a genuinely liked and well-known personality in the college.

These last three years have been a good time for Jane. She has had a terrific social life, making many friends, both on the college magazine team which she has helped to produce, as well as in the drama group. In fact she is playing an important role in a play due to be put on in the arts centre at the college in only a week's time, part of the drama group's third-term programme.

"I think Jane is going to be really good myself. I only hope, though, she's going to know her lines properly by the first night."

John Cameron, the producer of the play, drained his glass, and sat looking thoughtfully at it for a moment.

"The only thing is, John, I would be careful about pressurising her. I reckon that's what caused her to storm off like that. She is actually extremely worried about her finals, you know. And she has got a lot to think about at the moment."

Penny knows a great deal about Jane's recent problems. Penny is Jane's best friend. They shared a room together in their first year, and they hit it off right from day one. Jane really values someone to confide in. And quite honestly she knows it is just what she needs at the moment.

"Don't give me that, Penny. Everyone knows Jane's going to get a first. She is the best student in her year by far. Jane's a high flyer all right, always has been. No wonder she has been offered that job in Fleet Street. And there aren't many opportunities like that on offer. Still, I suppose I know what you mean. She *has* been behaving a bit funny lately."

As Jane sits there quietly in the front seat, she has to admit she *is* feeling unsettled. She feels tired, yet at the same time her mind is racing.

"That's two meals I've missed today. I can't keep on pretending I'm on a diet. I simply don't feel interested in eating at all. I wonder if I am going anorexic? Can't be! I just feel sick all the time. I wish I could curl up in a little ball and go to sleep. And maybe the whole world would go away: exams and jobs and living up to other people's expectations. I want to be out of it."

As the car speeds through the town, the thoughts simply flash through Jane's mind as swiftly as the scene viewed through the windscreen in front of her changes by the moment. Journey's end will be more revision, a late night, poor sleep and an early morning start.

"Sometimes I think revising is a waste of time. I know everybody expects me to do well. But what if I don't make it? I might even fail. I haven't really done enough work to do well. It is not my fault there have been so many other things to do. People don't realise it takes a long time for a broken relationship to heal. You can't just pick yourself up overnight. I'm fed up with other people expecting me to be brilliant. A front runner. Top of the class. I'm not. *I'm just me.* They don't understand how many changes I'll have to make if I take that Fleet Street job. The standard is so high. I don't think I'll cope. I'm so worried. I'm simply putting on a front for everyone. I'm *pretending* to be myself. I feel I could cry."

That thought of having to put on an act to be *herself* – so unsettled does Jane feel, brings it all on. A few gentle drops at first, then uncontrollably Jane begins to sob and sob and sob.

Jane's friend watches carefully out of the corner of her eye, as she skilfully manoeuvres the car through the traffic. After a moment rummaging through her bag she hands over a tissue. In a strange way, for such a small gesture, Jane finds it almost comforting.

Pause for Thought

You may well recognise something of yourself or your own experience in either Sarah, George or Jane's experience here. The difficulties they are facing are common ones, though there are many others of course. We will keep in touch with these three, and follow their progress as they try and cope with their difficulties. For the moment, it will be a good idea to ask what we can learn from the basic facts we have discovered about them.

Diagnosing the Trouble

When our lives come under pressure, the very first step in trying to help ourselves is to aim to be clear about the cause or causes of our difficulties. If a car chugs to a halt at the side of the road – the sensible thing is to have a quick check of the gauge to see whether it has run out of petrol. Discovering the cause enables us to face the issues properly, and do something about them. As any doctor will tell you, unless you get the diagnosis right you cannot be sure of a cure.

As far as anxiety and stress are concerned, it is our *reaction* to those causes which matters most. Some people seem to cope perfectly adequately with a new baby, extra responsibility at work or a big exam. Others do not. It is the reaction to causes which appears to be the important factor. Nonetheless, we have to seek out the cause, the stress or anxiety factor, first of all. That is definitely stage one.

Knowing Me

When we are out looking for causes, we often look to external factors like what is going on at work, or a financial situation or whatever. Yet in seeking for causes, the more we know about ourselves, the more we really know just what makes us tick, the better we will do at actually putting our finger on the real issues at stake. More will be said about this later. But for the moment here is an example.

Will the Real Me Please Stand Up?

I may be anxious about a new job. I certainly would not be the first person to be unsettled at the prospect of beginning a new piece of work, with new people to meet and get to know, and so much new information and ways of working to learn.

But if I realise I have quite a poor view of myself and my abilities, a low self-image as it is sometimes called, then my anxiety about the new situation may not be related quite so much to the job itself as I might at first imagine.

It may be that I am perfectly capable, according to my ability, to do quite as well in that new job as anybody else. It may also be that there is an annoying little whisper in my ear that I am not really good enough to do it. Like I am not good enough, honestly, at anything else. I know I am a failure; or so I often persuade myself.

The great fear is, that if I do make a hash of the job when I start, then the truth will be out. Everyone will know I am a failure, a no-good. What I always suspected about myself will be acknowledged by everyone – basically I'm rubbish. Hence the anxiety.

So if we are searching for causes, the root cause there is not so much the new job, but the deep concern bred by the low self-image. It is knowing the real me which matters.

How Do I Tick?

Supposing I understand the way I tick. I *recognise* I have this tendency to undervalue myself. Then I can go to work on my *attitudes*. I can face this low view of myself – which in turn will help much to deal with my anxiety about the new job situation.

We have to diagnose the trouble by seeking out the cause. Remembering to look at *ourselves*, as well as external circumstances, as a prelude to the cure. It is finding out what's going on under the bonnet, before you blame the road surface.

The more knowledge we have of ourselves, the more accurate our assessment of the cause. It is then we can look more constructively at what our reaction is, and begin to deal with it.

Sometimes the cause is simple and obvious. Other times, it is more complex and hidden – of which more later.

So What of our Three Friends?

Sarah, George and Jane are all going through it in their different ways. Though it is unwise to be too clinical, it appears as though Sarah's situation seems an equal mix of stress and anxiety, whereas George's situation appears to be laden mainly with stress factors alone. Jane by contrast is plain anxious, and we can all understand and feel for her. All of them are suffering, finding their lives pretty tough at the moment.

There is of course a kind of vicious circle at work in all this. As your fears increase about something, so the sense of felt pressure mounts, and you find yourself less and less capable of managing, coping, and facing the issues concerned. It is like having a string of late nights. You're tired during the day time, so everything takes longer, you *need* the extra time to do everything you have to do, so you never succeed in catching up on your sleep, you get more tired, and so on . . .

Sarah obviously has her hands more than full. There are the natural anxieties about Peter, and managing financially; the concerns about a changed lifestyle, and loss of friends and a social life. And then there is the sheer pressure of everything that has to be done: propping up Peter, washing Daniel's nappies, the night-time feeds, trying to manage the house. Stress and anxiety come together – and being bad friends, seem to make each other worse. Unless, of course, something is done.

We would all like to move in and change the external circumstances – a job for Peter, a friend's offer to help clean the house, and a magic wand to enable Daniel to sleep through the night! But we *do not* have that power.

It is as plain as daylight that George's life is overbusy. Though it is true that others seem to manage all right, he is obviously under pressure.

George is a very conscientious man, but he does not seem to be able to manage his stress very easily. Hence the arguments, the headaches and the unsettled feeling. Is George secretly fighting a job that he is unwilling to openly admit he hates? Is he taking on too much? What is really going on?

What about Jane? She managed fine with a fairly full schedule right up to exam time. It was only then she realised the little work she had done for finals to get the result she wanted. The anxiety is an obvious consequence. It is complicated by the fact of this offer of a quite prestigious job. It raises powerful questions of who she really is and where she is going in life. Is this job really her? What price turning such an offer down? Now we can see why Jane needed that paper handkerchief . . .

It's Not What You See, It's the Way You See It

How can *we* help? How can these people help *themselves*? Much can be done through changing attitudes. It is the way you see things which counts. And of course we need *strength* to change our attitudes. Christians rightly underline the power which comes direct from God through Jesus Christ, a power which does enable us to change our attitudes, break with old patterns of behaviour, and provides us with resources for growth and direction for the future. So any discussion of the way we change attitudes is going to involve us in looking seriously at how God enables us to grow and change and become more like the supreme example of Jesus himself.

For the moment, it is now time for us to seek to understand more precisely what anxiety and stress actually are, before we can talk in any detail about changing the attitudes which give rise to these states, and the resources that are available from God to help make those changes possible.

Chapter Two

THE NATURE OF ANXIETY

Anxiety takes many forms. Often the feelings involve:
- A deep uncertainty about the future
- Questions like "Will I cope?"
- An overwhelming sense of panic
- An inner awareness of shame
- Sometimes very specific fears
- Often just a vague but real sense of being plain worried

Everyone Faces It

Remember Jane. She was worried about exams which were coming up, and what the offer of a new job, which could well be bigger than her capabilities, might mean for her future. Or Sarah. What would happen if Peter remained unemployed for a long time? Would they manage? How would they afford all those bits and pieces they need to buy for Daniel? It *is* true, everyone faces anxiety – at some point along the way.

We have seen already that anxiety is related to fear. And it is time now to go into this in a little more detail. For when we understand just what anxiety is, we are much better placed to handle it. We may never be able to banish anxiety for ever. But on the other hand we can learn what to do about it if we understand how it begins to grow and take its hold over us in the first place.

None of Us Likes Green-Eyed Monsters

All of us have fears of various sorts. Some are common to everyone, like the fear of death. Others are more "specialised" like an intense dislike of spiders. Mostly, we are not particularly conscious of our inner fears. That is, until something happens to trigger a reaction within us, which sends the fear bouncing up towards the surface. And then it all begins to come out. Our fears are like horrid green-eyed monsters. We would rather not have anything to do with them. But sometimes they force themselves upon us.

A Day in the Life of . . . Sarah

When Peter came back home that day so despondent that work was still not available, he didn't appreciate the effect on Sarah.

That evening, when they were sitting up in bed reading, Sarah suddenly put her magazine down and sat silently for a moment. Then, slowly and quietly, measuring the weight of her words, she said: "Peter, darling, how are we going to manage over these next weeks, until you get another job?"

"You tell me, sweetheart. I don't know."

"But what about Daniel? How are we going to afford new clothes for him. It is getting so much colder now. There is no central heating in his bedroom. We need to buy a fan heater, some proper little woollens. Where are we going to get the money?"

"I don't know, Sarah."

"Peter, can't you at least understand, I'm worried?"

There was a pause.

"I am too, Sarah."

Peter was already asleep when Sarah let the tears pour out quietly into the softness of her pillow.

Fitting the Pieces Together

It is a difficult situation for them both to be involved in. Yet it was helpful when the health visitor enabled Sarah to fit some of the pieces together. They were talking about Sarah's family background. And when the health visitor asked about Sarah's childhood, Sarah had replied in rather more detail than she had meant to mention.

"Daddy was a technician in a power station, but he became ill with a lung complaint. It left him so breathless that in the end he had to give up work altogether, when he was only forty-five. As you know, he died not long after that. But though Mummy tried so hard to provide for us, money was always incredibly tight. And I often used to see Mummy tearful because she wasn't able to give us what other children had at school. So I resolved, even when I was quite small, I'd never let any family of mine get into a situation like that."

Sarah paused for a moment, biting her lip. "If I'm honest, that's why I went for that secretarial job. It was stupid of me to lie about my qualifications. I feel so guilty now. But it was so well paid. I hoped to be able to save up enough to see us through a rainy day, though I never thought this would happen to us. It is almost all gone now. But I'm terrified of ever getting into a situation again, like when we were young ..."

Learning the Lesson

Anxiety feeds on our fears. Sarah is feeling that awful sense of helplessness. But we can see already how the hidden fear of "poverty", which is based very much on the real experience of Sarah's past, has been triggered off by Peter's redundancy. And it has bounced up like a green-eyed monster, menacing and threatening, to cause poor Sarah real anxiety.

"It is all happening again. How will we cope? With Peter's health, and my exhaustion, it could destroy us in the end. *Then* what would happen to Daniel?"

The lesson here to learn is that we all carry around with us the baggage of our fears, rational and irrational, usually based on the attitudes and experiences which have made up our past. Because they *are* fears, and therefore breed uncomfortable emotions, most of us do not like to acknowledge them. So their ugly heads tend to get pushed down, ignored, or even strenuously avoided. But they are there all right, big and small, common and uncommon. And we experience *anxiety* when those fears are triggered off by a thought, an action or an event over which we exert no final control.

Let's be Personal

Are you unsure of *your* fears? Your most personal, inner concerns? Even the one greatest fear, which most causes you discomfort and pain in life? I expect you are, at least in some measure. We are going to think later about how, with God's help, we can deal with those fears, and therefore cope better with anxiety.

But for a few moments now, let's be personal. This would be a good time to put this book down, find a piece of paper, a quiet spot and a comfortable chair, and think about those fears which are real for you.

For some of us this *can* be uncomfortable. But if you want to learn to deal with your rebel emotions, this is where you have to begin. Could I suggest you write down what you consider your greatest fears, being as specific as you like, even though some may turn out only to be quite vague, or even irrational. They are still fears, so they matter – because they are part of you! We are not talking so much about the ordinary little worries which are not so troublesome. The very minor anxieties which do not stay long, and hardly bother you. We are thinking here about the deeper inner concerns. Those things which really make you fearful.

When you have finished, keep the piece of paper in a safe place, because we shall need to use it again, to learn what to do with them, how to handle the fears which turn themselves so easily and inconveniently into full-blown anxiety.

Take your time. And here is a suggested prayer you can use, to ask God's help: "Lord, thank you that you know me through and through. You know everything about me, even the things I am reluctant to accept about myself. Thank you, then, that you can help me uncover what my inner fears actually are. Please do this now, as I sit and ponder these things. And may this be just the beginning of your re-strengthening of my life, as I learn through your help to overcome these difficulties. In Jesus' name. Amen."

In taking that opportunity to have a good think about your own fears, you may or may not have discovered anything new. Equally, you perhaps have discovered the *intensity* with which those fears are variously invested within yourself; just how fearful you feel about the issues you have been thinking of. That is important too, and we shall come back to that soon as well.

For the moment we can make this distinction. Fear is the attitude of dread which we have fixed within us – usually about those situations over which we can exert no final control. That is why the future is such a common component in fear awareness.

Anxiety is simply the extension of fear. It is when an actual situation gives rise to emotions, which feed on the inner uncertainties, fuelled by the "hidden" fears ticking away inside us, those deep uncertainties which are sleeping so lightly, just waiting to be triggered by a similar event on the surface of things. Just like Sarah's panic about Peter, with that hidden fear of a re-run of her childhood deprivations.

So our fears are *latent anxieties*. Like alien seeds beneath the surface of the soil, we only notice their presence when the weeds spring up from them, forcing their way into the daylight world and spoiling the landscape all around. And because our fears are simply waiting for an opportunity to latch on to some suitable situation above ground, the best way forward is to recognise *our fears need to be faced, accepted and dealt with.*

Facing our Fears

The problem with anxiety is that it invariably distorts the truth. That may sound unfair at first. After all, who is not concerned when their husband loses his job, or when exam time is looming? But truth is bigger than simply the bald facts of any situation.

The dominant feeling in anxiety is helplessness. We cannot control the situation. It is out of our hands. We know what we would like to happen, but are not able, for various reasons, to make it turn out like that.

The real truth is we do not live in an impersonal universe. We are not on our own, the plaything of the impersonal forces all around us. We have a God who cares deeply about what happens to us. And more than that, he knows what is best for us. In a real sense, he is in overall control of the world he has made.

We cannot of course treat God like a genie in a lamp, and get him to order events in the way we would like them to go. There are other people in this world who have to be considered too! On the other hand, it does not mean we cannot ask God for things, trust in his loving, fatherly care for us, and believe in the end his purposes are best. Of course God can change events as well as the way we react to them.

How Should We Face Our Fears?

The only way to face our fears realistically is by faith. Faith in a God who made the world and who has made us. He has demonstrated his power *in* this world by actually bringing Jesus back from the dead. Jesus' resurrection is regarded by the New Testament writers as the standard demonstration of God's power and authority. We *are* talking about a God who can *do* things. And even more, this God sent Jesus in the first place to be nothing less than a Saviour for us, who offers forgiveness, a new start in life, and strength and power for the Holy Spirit to overcome – yes, even our anxieties and fears.

The place of faith is going to need a little more explanation. We cannot replace our fears with faith, until we are somewhat more clear what is going on deep down within us at this level of fear and uncertainty.

Assessing Our Fears

The teaching of Jesus is full of insights into fear and anxiety. Mainly because Jesus, understanding us perfectly, knows how paralysing the plain experience of worry can be for us.

"No-one can serve two masters. Either he will hate the one, and love the other, or he will be devoted to the one and despise the other. You cannot serve both God and Money. Therefore I tell you, do not worry about your life, what you will eat or drink; or about your body, what you will wear. Is not life more important than food, and the body more important than clothes? Look at the birds of the air; they do not sow or reap or store away in barns, and yet your heavenly Father feeds them. Are you not much more valuable than they? Who of you by worrying can add a single hour to his life?" Matthew 6:24–27

The first thing Jesus is asking us to do, is to be *realistic* about our fears. We cannot necessarily remove them altogether, but we can prevent them from causing us anxiety or worry by disarming their power over us. And the first step in that direction is to do with realism.

One of Those Nights

When Sarah did eventually get off to sleep she did not seem to sleep very deeply. She simply went over in her mind, half dreaming, half waking, these same old worries and concerns. She had hardly been asleep half an hour when Daniel needed his two o'clock feed. Sarah had been so unsettled with him, that it seemed to take an age to wind him, and get *him* back to sleep.

It was one of those nights. Peter was restless. Daniel started crying at four. Sarah jumped out of bed immediately to put him right. Back in bed again, she only managed a little sleep before Daniel was wanting his breakfast at six o'clock! She would have gone back to bed again except Peter was up making coffee and Sarah could not bear to be alone with her thoughts.

"Peter is never going to get another job, ever. He's sick. We won't be able to pay the mortgage. We'll have to move. I'll never manage. I can't cope. I can't face it."

Respecting Fears

It *is* going to be all right. Yet that is the last thing Sarah feels at the moment. On the other hand, although it is helpful sometimes to be simply reassuring, telling Sarah, "Pull yourself together" or "Every cloud has a silver lining" or even such a profound scriptural truth as "All things work together for good . . ." may only produce a plate arriving missile-like in your direction. And thoroughly deserved too. We must learn to listen and respect what people are feeling.

Do Not Argue with Others' Emotions

Many of us have faced the agony of some particularly anxious situation, only to find some well-meaning person trying to talk us out of the emotions, arguing with the way we feel. Whereas the way to be realistic is first to look at the issues themselves, and ask the question: what is going on here? Respecting the emotions as an indication of the deeply-felt need of the person involved.

Take Sarah. She is getting to the panic stage, because of Peter's situation. So we must take what she is feeling seriously. Yet at the same time, let us stand back and try and be objective. Peter *is* capable and resourceful. It is true he is very down at the moment. But why should he be like that for ever? Sarah knows as well as anyone else in the family, that if they were prepared to move, Peter could get a job in the garage where his father is the manager. So if the worst came to the worst, they would hardly starve. Is this all as bad as it seems?

Often we need someone else's help to see things clearly again. How valuable it is to talk things through.

Getting it into Focus

A further step in helping us to restore the perspective is to give a thought to our hopes and aspirations. They are the flip side of our fears. Getting these into focus, again will help us to be much clearer about our fears. For fear is the opposite of hope. And if we know what hopes our fears may be threatening, we can assess again the reasonableness of those hopes, with direct effect and implications for the fears too.

You may find it instructive to get that piece of paper again, and make a list of your hopes. The hopes for your family, for yourself, for your future and so on. When you have done that, ask yourself are they realistic? Would I be prepared to put up with anything less? Then think about what you know of Jesus, and how many limitations he was prepared to put up with. Go back to that passage in the Sermon on the Mount, quoted earlier, and compare your hopes *and* fears with what Jesus says there.

Notice that Jesus asks this pertinent question: What do we achieve by worrying? Worrying about something will not be able to add even a single hour to our life. So why worry?

The answer is we do. Don't we know it! But Jesus' point is we need not. We need not worry nearly so much if we learn several basic lessons: to be realistic about our fears; to accept the situations in which we are involved; and, most importantly, to develop faith in the Heavenly Father's loving, understanding, caring provision for us. To which points we should now turn.

Overcoming our Fears

Peter did eventually go to the vicar. It was the health visitor's idea. Quite by chance, it seemed, she met Peter by the post office. She had remarked that Peter was looking tired, and he said he was as worried as Sarah was about the future. Then he said how valuable Sarah had found talking everything through, and how grateful he was to her for that. To which he had received the reply: "Talking is helpful, Peter. I know you go to church. Have you ever thought of having a word with Mr Coombes, the vicar? He's a family man like yourself, and he's very understanding."

Peter managed a smile, and they parted. But when Sarah was in the other room that afternoon, he phoned the vicar, and was reassured by the welcoming attitude he received.

Peter saw the vicar several times, gaining in confidence on each occasion. Sarah was also invited along eventually, to help Mr Coombes help Peter, or that was how the vicar put it.

They talked openly about their fears. And hearing themselves ventilate those almost hidden concerns really helped. They were able to be much more realistic about the way they were reacting to their present circumstances. Sarah particularly saw that she was almost pre-programmed to get panicky whenever any insecure situation developed, because of the memories of unhappy times as a child after her father's death. And also to a certain extent her expectations were a little fixed and unrealistic. If it came to it, after all, they could move. Even if it were all rather inconvenient . . .

You would think it would be good to fight against something like unemployment. In some obvious ways of course it is. But Peter, and to a certain extent Sarah, were fighting the stigma of it all.

They were having difficulty in accepting the situation, and in some ways they were their own worst enemies, believing that they were *no* good. Failures. When they were open and honest about it, after discussion, they realised this too was causing them considerable discomfort. They were able, with help, to get this much more into perspective.

Perhaps the most lasting help came from recognising that deep personal security comes from giving God our undivided loyalty. James Coombes explained it this way to them:

"That is why Jesus says you cannot serve two masters. You have to choose. Either you are going to go all out for material things, that is what Jesus means by Money. Or you'll give God your total allegiance. And after all, since he is able to look after creatures like the birds who have no capacity to care for themselves, he should be able to look after people like us. It is not that material things are not important, but we have to learn to put God first. The key to it is understanding that God is our father – it starts from the moment we trust Jesus as our Saviour. And as a loving father, he is hardly likely to give up on us. He'll provide for all our needs, in just the way he knows is lastingly best for us."

Both Sarah and Peter took this seriously. For it is often when we feel vulnerable in life that we are most open to God's help. But what we learn in the rough times, we have to store up and remember to practise in the good times – when our need of God's help may not seem quite so acute.

The words which Peter found most helpful were those which he noticed when he was studying the passage the vicar had shown him later that night. "Seek first his kingdom and his righteousness, and all these things will be given to you as well. Therefore do not worry about tomorrow, for tomorrow will worry about itself. Each day has enough trouble of its own." Matthew 6:33–34

Peter worked out again with Sarah what the vicar had pointed out. There were two priorities, a promise, and then a command.

First to seek God's kingdom. That means to genuinely want God first in your life, and to let him take over the running of things.

Second to live righteously. That is to live and behave in ways which are pleasing to God. It means giving up and taking on. But it is worth it in the end. It means sticking to God's rules which genuinely bring freedom.

The promise is that when we put God first, showing by our

behaviour we really mean business, God puts his cards straight on to the table and pledges himself to meet our material needs. It is only when the spiritual is right, that the material works out properly as well. Christianity is no credit card religion, an instant passport to success, wealth and happiness. But at the same time God wants to meet our needs, as we trust him. And he alone knows finally what is best for us.

So the command is obvious. If you are going to trust God actively, worry is plainly and simply – useless. I must get on with today. It has enough to do. Leave tomorrow to God . . .

There was still much to sort out. But the attitudes were changing. And even Daniel slept well that night.

Action Point

Something needs to be done about our fears. In the light of what we have considered so far, here are some suggestions. Remind yourself of what you wrote down about your own inner concerns.

Realism

Come to terms with the worst possible outcome. Supposing you did become terminally ill, or you lost your partner or that very close friend. Maybe you were discovered not to be the capable person you have always wanted to be, while in your heart knowing it was all a sham. Face it! Accept it might happen. Don't run away. If you stay put, there is so much that can be done – that you can do too – to make sure you will manage. It is like accepting your own mortality. We all have to do this. As we are all going to die, we may as well save ourselves the trauma of worrying about it and get on with living. You need to ventilate your fears. Talk them over. Find yourself accepted and not told you are stupid. And you need God's help too.

Is There Anyone to Turn To?

If you are really going to go to work on those fears – maybe your deepest number one fear – then how can God help? How can he make a difference? Part of the help comes from recognising that fear makes us feel vulnerable, and it leaves us feeling powerless and threatened.

So is there anyone to turn to? Imagine your fear as actual fact. What would make the difference to your sense of panic, the jangled emotions, that deeply unsettling sensation of insecurity and dis-ease within? Especially if you cannot remove the possibility of the feared situation itself.

The very last words Jesus said to his followers according to Matthew's account in his gospel are:

"Surely, I will be with you always, to the very end of the age."
Matthew 28:20

It is a promise. I will be with you always. There *is* someone to turn to. And we need to learn to turn over our fears to Jesus, so he can heal us from the powerful and painful hold they exert over us.

The Way Out

A practical way to find that way out from these fears we have been discussing, which are the building blocks, the foundation stones, of our day-to-day anxieties – is to bring our fears, however irrational or poignant, to God in prayer.

If you wrote down your own thoughts on that piece of paper, perhaps I can suggest you prayerfully bring those fears to God in the next few moments, or when you are settled and ready. You can tell him all your deepest worries, however strange that may feel. He understands, and loves you. And remember, when you have told him those things, Jesus has promised to be with you – always.

He has promised to be there in all situations, however painful. He will be with you as you cope with unemployment.

He will be with you should you face rejection. He will be with you if that relationship breaks down. He will be with you as you grow old; as you lie there waiting for an operation in the hospital. And more than that, he will be with you when you die.

Faith means taking hold of this promise. You have to keep working on it day after day. As you go to bed. As you wake up in the morning. The issue is this: Are we alone? Or is there someone there to whom we can turn? Anxiety is a paralysing and painful experience. The only way to deal with it adequately is to recognise that it is our attitudes, rather than the external situations themselves, which are the real cause of our trouble. And since we do have someone to turn to, there is a final way out – or at the very least a way forward – in dealing with our anxiety, knowing God's help and, through his Spirit, Jesus' presence with us.

Chapter Three

THE SHAPE OF STRESS

Stress is sometimes confused with anxiety. The confusion is more to do with the word itself, for it is true that anxiety produces distress within us. But stress as such is more to do with *pressures* from *outside* rather than from fears *within*, and how we react to them.

In this chapter we are going to deal with the shape of stress and how we react to the pressures going on round about us.

Many people these days lead fairly frantic lives, trying to pack into twenty-four hours far more activity and responsibility than is really fair to our frail human frame. No wonder our bodies object, and give us hints we can feel or see when everything is getting too frenetic. Sometimes a change or interruption to our routine can come as an equal shock to the system.

"Say Aaah, Please"

It was the doctor peering down George's throat. It was not just George's headaches. When the doctor asked George if there was "anything else", it turned out George felt something of a medical wreck!

"Say Aaah, please."

"Aaah . . ."

"Thank you, Mr Saunders."

The doctor paused to jot something down in his notes. "You can get yourself dressed now."

George felt a sense of relief. The doctor had looked at his throat and checked him over thoroughly. He buttoned up his shirt and replaced his tie, as the doctor had also taken the trouble to examine his heart and lungs and have a press around his stomach to see if anything was wrong.

"I can't find much to worry about except the mouth ulcers. And they should clear up soon. Wash your mouth out three times a day with this solution I'll give you, and in a few days everything will be fine."

George felt relieved, but still in some ways a bit edgy.

"I am sorry to go on about it, but can you tell me what is it that is giving me this mild burning pain in my stomach, and making my heart seem as though it is racing all the time?"

The doctor was silent for a moment.

"Everything all right at home?"

George nodded.

"Are you worried about anything, Mr Saunders?"

George did not feel he could say. Still it was not so much worry, as being dog-tired. There was such a lot to do.

"Come back and see me in a week's time, if you're still feeling the same, and we'll have another chat."

The doctor smiled as they shook hands and George walked back through the surgery waiting room.

"At least he was thorough," George thought, feeling more relaxed, as he climbed into the car. "Look at the time! I must rush into town before the shops close for lunch, and buy some more weed killer."

George spent the next half hour careering round the stores before arriving home feeling three quarters whacked. He made a start on his lunch, hardly acknowledging Mary and the children.

At the surgery, the doctor had written a reminder to himself on George's notes: "Stress symptoms?" He would make time to discuss it with him next week, if George needed to come back.

So What is Stress?

Stress is something we experience either physically or
mentally or both. It is often defined as the reaction of our
mind and body to change: producing pressure. We could say
there is normal stress and abnormal stress. "Normal stress"
is simply the pressure to get on and do things, when there is
much to be achieved. It does not harm us because it is mainly
providing a spur to purposeful activity, which is perfectly
reasonable to manage. However, "abnormal stress" is more
discomforting, because the "changes" involved produce
more pressure on us than we can happily handle.

These changes might be, as in George's case, an increased
workload; for a student, the extra demands of study at exam
time; for a young mother, the broken nights from seeing to the
needs of young children. All are a departure from our own
personal "norm" with which we cope best, a significant
change from our own optimum ability to cope mentally and
physically with the pressures that come our way.

I am an Individual

We are all made differently, and are the product of the
influences of our upbringing and experiences. So it is not
surprising we should all have different levels of stress
tolerance – our ability to cope with pressure. That is why an
important feature of learning to manage our stress is to know
ourselves thoroughly, our strengths as well as our limitations.

Go beyond our own personal level of stress tolerance, and
we will recognise the onset of abnormal stress. As the
pressures mount up, and *dis*tress begins to manifest itself
physically, mentally and even spiritually.

What are the Signs?

Quite honestly, any doctor will tell you that stress can appear
in many different ways, in terms of physical signs. Yet

physical signs have their emotional counterparts. Human beings are not impersonal machines. Here are a few of the more common physical and emotional reactions:

- Headaches
- Upset stomach or indigestion
- Backache
- Sinking feeling inside
- Loss of concentration
- Reduced tolerance; irritability, and bad temper
- Tenseness
- Self-pity
- Forgetfulness
- Inability to make decisions easily

Can you add to the list from your own experience? How does your body react when the heat is on, when things are getting too much? What are the kinds of emotions you go through when you are beginning to come under stress?

Recognise Your Signs

It is important to know yourself. To know your own body and mind, in order to look after yourself properly. That is why it is as well to be able to recognise your own signs of stress as they manifest themselves physically and through your moods, and mood changes. Those physical and emotional signs are the warning shots our body and mind throw out at us to make sure we are aware of what is happening to us, just like the warning lights on a car dashboard, when the engine is getting overheated, or it is running dangerously low on oil. These are the safety measures God has built into our design. And it is up to us to be responsible and respond quickly when the lights start flashing. Of course to do that – and we are all different – each of us has to become aware what are our *own* stress symptoms, and, knowing them, act accordingly.

Stop, Look, Listen

So let us stop for a moment, have a good look at ourselves, and ask what it is our bodies are saying to us.

A piece of paper and a pencil may be helpful again. Think back to a time when you felt you were definitely under stress. Did you have any physical symptoms – headache, stomach trouble and so on? What about emotionally? How did you feel? What words would you use to describe your emotions? How were you "different" from your normal self? Could other times of stress add to your findings?

Write your notes down on the paper. Don't worry if you cope quite easily with stress and therefore have little to report. You are a fortunate person! But if you have written a few thoughts down, the chances are you have your own stress profile to hand. That is to say you have isolated those warning signs which from time to time flash away with their message that all is not well. Having recognised them, you can take action as soon as they make their appearance, before the stress itself becomes too much to bear.

This Is Your Life

Recognising the warning signs may be very useful in knowing what to do once the stress has appeared. But what about the factors which give rise to stress in the first place?

We have noted that stress is the reaction of the mind and body to change. It is our reaction to the pressure produced by certain kinds of changes. Again, since all of us are different, we all have our own personal list of stress-inducing factors, factors which are guaranteed to make us feel miserably uncomfortable whenever they make their unwelcome appearance on our physical and mental timetable.

Some More Personal Analysis

Give yourself some moments to think. Then jot down what

you consider are the factors which cause stress for you in particular. You will be thinking no doubt about family, relationships, work, lifestyle and so on. Be careful not to confuse this with anxieties. You are thinking about what divergences from your normal sense of well-being, cause you *extra* pressure, leading to stress. Not about those inner fears which external situations trigger into anxieties. Again it will be instructive to do a "This is Your Life" on yourself, and review some of your major (and minor) times of stress experience from over the years. Do take time now to do this.

When you have done that (and if you do want to learn to manage your own stress better, I think you will find the few minutes the exercise takes very well spent), keep the notes you have made in a safe place. For the present simply use the material to be more comprehensively aware of your own personal make-up and what it is which makes you tick in this area of stress.

The Domains of Stress

All of us know that pressures come at us from practically every area of life. *Changes* upset our physical and emotional routine, and it takes us time to *adapt* to changing and new situations. Similarly *conflict* upsets our equilibrium. It *challenges* us at several different levels, and we need extra energy and reserves to tolerate and/or accept the need for changes within ourselves.

This quartet of change, conflict, challenge and adaptation we see variously at work in the four main areas where stress most commonly appears. These are: family, relationships, work and lifestyle.

We shall have a look at each of these areas in turn, when we have seen a little more of the Saunders family in action.

After the Storm

George *thought* it was going to rain as he drove back home

from town, but he was not prepared for a downpour like this. It had simply come over grey with a few rain clouds when he had pulled the car into the drive. Now, sitting there, painfully conscious of the fact that he was late again for lunch, George was lost in his thoughts as he spooned his meal – when a crack of thunder brought him immediately to his senses, like the sudden sharpness of a hypodermic needle. George looked up to see the hail stones pouring down, their constant beat upon the french windows sounding like machine-gun fire at a distance.

"Dad, could you take me over to John's house this afternoon? I was going to catch a bus over, but I'll get really soaked in this." Amanda smiled at her father.

"Wait and see if it stops . . ." George replied.

It did not, which in itself made George cross because the grass had not been cut for such a long time, and he had particularly wanted and planned to do it this afternoon. And all that time spent searching for the weed killer, making himself late for lunch, and now none of it was going to get done . . . At least he had brought home some work from the office and would be able to get on with that.

Driving Amanda over to John's house, the other side of town, George began to mutter under his breath.

"What are you saying, Daddy?" enquired Amanda. George's hands tightened on the steering wheel.

"It's these wretched Saturday afternoon drivers. I shouldn't think they drive at any other time. They seem to emerge and vent their collective incompetence just at the moment when I need to get quickly through the town centre."

Amanda did not say anything. She could not see it was anything to get hot under the collar about.

"What a plain daft, unthought-through development this new one-way system is! It's twice as slow as things were before. I sometimes think we have got a bunch of buffoons on our town council."

Amanda thought it was time to change the subject.

"Dad, can I ask you about this evening?"

"What, Amanda?"

"Well you see, Dad, John is having this party. And I promised I'd help him clean up afterwards, because his parents are coming home from holiday tomorrow. So will it be all right if you don't wait up for me? Because I may be back a bit later than usual, probably not till twelve thirty, maybe one o'clock."

It was like a red rag to a bull. Though the driver in front got it first, if only for braking rather suddenly. George leaned on his horn angrily and ferociously.

"No, Amanda, it will not be all right. While you live in our house you'll do what we say. Ten thirty is quite late enough, and you'll not be in any later. And what, may I ask, does John plan to get up to while his parents are away? Does his father know he is planning to have a party while they are not there to supervise it?"

The rain started to increase in force, so George flicked the windscreen wipers into fast mode. "John's parents didn't say he couldn't, Dad. Anyway I've promised I'll help. Mum said it would be all right."

"Well I say it's not. And that's final."

The pulsating wipers swished away the constant downpour of rain and hail on the steamed-up glass of the car's windscreen.

"Oh come on, Dad. You don't expect John to clear up all by himself."

George actually felt like telling Amanda a home truth or two. But he did not. He took a deep breath, and said quietly and as calmly as he could manage: "OK, Amanda. You can stay until twelve and absolutely no later. Mind you behave yourself though. And I'll come and collect you at midnight."

George felt cross. He'd wanted an early night. He was so tired.

Amanda was jubilant.

"Mum was right . . . It's just a matter of choosing your moment."

Family Fortunes

The family is a major area of stress for most of us. If that sounds negative, it is not meant to, since it is our family which is made to bring us the greatest source of joy. If God has designed it so, then it is not surprising that since these relationships are so loaded with significance for us, then from time to time we will feel the pressure of change, conflict, challenge and adaptation.

This is obviously the case with George. When Amanda was a baby, she was the sweetest little darling you could imagine. George, like any parent, has had to adapt to the changes in both Amanda and Ben. Amanda is a teenager. She is in that transition stage between childhood and adulthood – and adapting to that change for George is as difficult as for any other parent.

There is often a lot of noise in families with teenage children, noise from record players, conversations, arguments. It is all stress-inducing. George finds this particularly difficult to cope with. But families provide other areas for potential stress: the relationship between a husband and wife; children to parents as well as parents to children.

Are you aware of the particular or potential stress areas in your family? It is good to give some thought to this, and try to be as specific as possible.

Wider Relationships

We have wider relationships, of course, than just our family provides, whether we are married or not. Romantic relationships can certainly cause stress. Yet the maintaining of simple friendships also brings pressure at times. Analyse your relationships in terms of the extent of change, conflict, challenge, adaptation, and you will see clearly the potential for stress our ordinary interactions can bring. Here are these four elements spelt out a little more fully.

CHANGE is part of life. At any one time, being creatures

of habit, we are used to coping with such and such an amount, done in such and such a way. Change puts all this on the line. Can we take more on? Are we prepared to do things in a different way?

CONFLICT can be both creative and destructive. It comes to us usually unwelcomely. It upsets our "normal" equilibrium. Am I in the wrong? Is "my way" of doing things under threat? Conflict threatens our sense of authority, even identity. That is why most people do not like it. Even though some conflict can turn out to be thoroughly positive, a spur to creative change.

CHALLENGE is the issue raised by change and conflict. Mentally we are all stuck in a rut. We have all settled for the most comfortable way of doing and seeing things. It takes us quite an effort to get settled in this way, and that is why challenge is so uncomfortable for us. It is like moving house. The thought of packing up all our bits and pieces yet again is discomforting to say the least. Yet challenge brings its promises. It can be as equally creative as negative and destructive, depending on the mindset involved.

ADAPTATION is something we have to cope with all the time, though whether we adapt quickly or thoroughly enough is another matter. Adaptation is best defined as the amount of distance we are prepared to move, either emotionally or physically, in response to the challenges raised by external change or conflict as they affect our lives.

Stressing the Question

How much *change* are you involved in at the moment? What kinds of *conflict* are involved? (Here is a situation where conflicts in your own mind are as important as external conflicts.) What are the *challenges* raised for you by these changes and conflicts? How are you responding – are you prepared and able to *adapt* to new situations? This kind of questioning will help you assess the stress factors for you in the various situations of stress, which are the normal domains of potential difficulty for most people. Take a moment to think this through. It is worth the effort!

Work, Work, Glorious Work

The truth is: work is anything but glorious when it gets too much for us. "George, you've been sitting there writing that report all afternoon. Won't you come and have some tea?"

Mary was frankly annoyed that George was bringing home work at weekends as well as in the evenings. But she tried to sound calm, as she knew George was under particular pressure at work.

"Can you give me fifteen minutes, Mary? And I'll be down soon." George started to write as fast as he could. He would try and finish it if he could.

Later George explained to Mary how very tired he felt at the moment; how difficult work had been this week with the senior partner still away; how he was hardly getting any break at lunchtime. And the work itself was becoming really tedious.

When Mary insisted George go and have a hot bath, and come down afterwards and watch the television, and that *she* would pick Amanda up at midnight – to her surprise, George agreed.

"Was your bath nice, George?" Mary asked as they began to watch the Saturday night film together. The fire was alight, and the room cosy and warm. The only reply she received was a couple of grunts. George had fallen asleep, and was beginning to snore nicely.

The increase in workload for George was a significant "change" for him at work. One that he was not adapting to particularly well, since he seemed to be resisting the challenge of altering his priorities. He could say no, if he wanted to. But that two-letter word does not seem to figure too prominently in his work vocabulary.

In another sense George was beginning to fight his work. He had convinced himself he was bored, unfulfilled. The drudgery of it all was getting him down. It had produced a conflict: the conflict between the way his work actually is, and the way George would like it to be.

If you are a working person, what are the stress factors of your situation? Can you recognise them? If you can isolate them it will be helpful. You will be able much better then to deal with them, before they start doing anything to you!

What a Lifestyle!

George was up early. He was determined to get the grass cut before church. With any luck he could get the weeding done too. He and Mary arrived at church with only two minutes to spare, even though George was supposed to be showing people to their seats that day. After the service was over, and George helped count the money from the collection, George and Mary dashed over to the tennis club for a pre-lunch drink with some friends.

It was a hectic day. Lunch at home, entertaining four colleagues and their wives from work. Then off to the park to watch Ben play football. Drop off Amanda to John's. Then a little more weeding. Wash the car. After that some more work on the report for Monday morning. All of which took him up to eleven o'clock when he could not keep his eyes open any longer.

The week which followed was a similar mad dash for the finishing line . . .

There *is* only so much you can fit into a day. And just as a composer will vary the pace of a piece of music, so we have to learn to be aware of the rhythm of our lives and pace ourselves accordingly.

This is where George was scoring badly. He was not realising the importance of adequate relaxation and sleep. He was packing in far more than was good for him. What was driving George?

In a moment we will examine the importance of our attitudes. But for now, how about *your* lifestyle? All work and no play makes Jack a dull boy. Are you finding a balance? Are you having enough time off? It may be the other way round, you may need to apply yourself harder. Laziness can bring its own kind of stress, felt in terms of sluggishness. But are you attending to a good balanced diet, with proper time set aside for meal times, recreation, sleep and so on? How are you pacing yourself at work? Are you rushing at everything like a bull in a china shop – or letting others propel you in the same way?

We ignore the principles God has built into our design at our peril. We see these principles working out clearly in the life of Jesus.

Jesus must have been in considerable demand throughout his public ministry: people requiring help from every quarter, invitations to speak, places to visit, people to see. Yet we never once see Jesus rushing anywhere. Often the gospel writers record that Jesus "withdrew" from the crowd. He would go off to a quiet place. He would pray. What can we learn from him?

- Jesus paced himself day by day, week by week.
- Jesus took adequate rest.
- Jesus ate sensibly. We often see him described at mealtimes.
- Jesus valued quiet.
- Jesus took recreation.
- Jesus prayed regularly.
- Jesus observed the Sabbath principle.

A Christian approach to lifestyle must take the example of Jesus seriously. Refusal to do so will inevitably give rise to stress symptoms. For the appearance of stress always implies a violation of the pattern for which we have been made.

It Depends How You Feel

The hidden world of our attitudes is an important factor in the experience of stress. We have mentioned that stress is our *reaction* to pressure. How we react depends on how we feel, or the attitudes we have hidden beneath the surface.

Broadly we might divide the attitudes relevant in this area into two categories: personality traits and expectations.

Personality Traits

Aspects of our personality can in certain circumstances be harbingers of stress, in that these personality traits are themselves in need of a certain amount of resolution.

An example would be the perfectionist personality. Many of us are like this. We prefer things in neat piles. Everything has to be just so. If not, we become uneasy and want to change the situation. We do not like muddle, and are unhappy if something is not done "properly". Very often perfectionists are quite aware of their personality and are very reasonable in their day-to-day expectations. Yet though they have learnt to live with their perfectionism, some situations can take them unawares.

The anxious personality similarly can experience stress as well as anxiety from his situation. Often those given to frequent worry find themselves so strenuously avoiding anxiety situations, that they end up by experiencing stress as a result instead!

Sometimes there is something over which we have become very angry, but have never had the chance to express that anger fully. Often the anger will want to push itself up, but will not be allowed by its reluctant owner. This itself is stressful, when the anger factor meets a potential stress factor. Explosions within are not only uncomfortable, but dangerous. Unexpressed anger is undesirable. We shall have a closer look in the next chapter.

Expectations

We may divide expectations into two parts: self-image and our "image" of others.

Self-image: the way we see ourselves is a primary issue in how we react to certain circumstances. The way we see ourselves should be taken together with the uneasy truce between the way we would like others to see us, and the way they in fact do. There are often circumstances when our self-image is at stake. Was it, for instance, significant that George was falling over himself to do the senior partner's work?

How about *your* self-image? How do you see yourself? Take five minutes to think over the way you see yourself. Ask yourself how you would like others to see you, and then compare it with how you think you actually are. Do not forget your conclusions – we shall want to return to these thoughts in the next chapter.

Our "image" of others: here is a potential area for trouble! We all have a picture in our minds of how those who are closest to us ought to be and to behave. We are idealists. When our friends/family fail to live up to our expectations, this can be a source of pain for us, even of stress. Equally, trying to compete with others or be like someone else can be a source of discomfort too.

George wants Amanda to be the sweet, obedient, bright and intelligent girl she was when she was ten. She has changed, but not George's expectations. It simply grates on him, Amanda wanting to stay out late at parties. In one sense of course there is a reasonable concern for Amanda's well-being. But what really animates George is his "image" of what he would like Amanda to be like. The gap between that image and reality is the cause of stress, at this level of the hidden world of attitudes – the way we feel.

Chapter Four

WHEN THE ROADS CONVERGE: STRESS AND ANXIETY TOGETHER

Although anxiety and stress can both be defined and experienced separately, often it is the case that several *different* factors go to make up any one situation. So anxiety and stress can and often do appear together.

Take, for example, a major illness. The illness itself may be very debilitating. The consequent pressures produce stress, not only for the sufferer, but perhaps also for the family, seeking to manage with the demands of a new and taxing situation. But anxiety can be involved too. "What is going to be the end of all this? Will I get better? What if I don't?" The family too may have similar concerns.

Is there then, a comprehensive way to respond to such issues, to minimise our discomfort, and take some steps forward? In order to do that we shall need some further insight into the way our attitudes undergird our reactions to various kinds of pressure, and into what constitutes the true basis of our values and security – we need a closer look at our foundations. What motivates us and makes us tick?

Time to Move On

The improvement is remarkable. Over these last few months Peter and Sarah have been much more settled in themselves.

Nothing has changed much in their circumstances, unfortunately, but their *attitude* has been so different.

It is true nonetheless that since they made their decision to move, they have had a few twinges of uncertainty.

Peter's father has found Peter a job at the garage, and has offered to lend them money to cover moving expenses. Yet Sarah finds it all so strange. As a couple, Peter's parents have never been anything but helpful and considerate towards them, but Sarah knows that Peter's previous wife was very much liked by his parents. When Peter and Sarah were first engaged, she found a photograph of Monica on the dressing-table in the spare room. Of course it was a mistake, but Sarah was understandably upset.

There really are some complications. Peter's nineteen-year-old son lives in the same town as Peter's parents. Sarah has only met him a couple of times, but he doesn't seem to want to know her.

Sarah looked forward to the move with a mixture of emotions. It was marvellous to think that in a week's time they would be back on a proper income again, and their worries about money over. But what a job the actual move would be. At least Peter was so much better, with so much more energy and "go" in him.

Sarah is strangely unable to admit, either to herself or Peter, the anxiety she feels about being near Peter's parents – or, more particularly, his former wife and his son Andrew. Peter has often said the past is past; and all his friends say he is quite a different person from those days. But somehow that makes no difference . . .

Peter is, in fact, sympathetic. He has an inkling of what *might* be on Sarah's mind, though he has not mentioned it. Instead he points to something he has been pondering over:

"I don't really feel too bothered about the move, in a way. I am looking forward to getting down to work. But perhaps that's the only possible area of worry for me. I do hope I'll cope OK. I've never sold cars in my life before. It is nice that Dad is there to refer to. But all the same, I'd rather stand on my own two feet if I can."

Peter smiles as he says it. It *is* clear he is feeling better.

"Darling, let's face it. It is such an exciting possibility. God has been so kind to us. He has answered our prayers, and guided us so far. He is not going to suddenly give up on us now!"

Sarah feels much more assured in her faith now. Hearing herself say those words and believing them, Sarah finds it difficult to account for the shiver of uncertainty she suddenly feels, when her eyes meet Peter's, as he smiles and takes her hand.

Road Works, Beware!

Whether we like it or not, there are always things going on under the surface. It is not so much that we need to go off and dig up the road to find out. It is simply to accept that beneath the ground level of our everyday experience, there is much going on. Certainly we should be informed of what is happening, and sometimes it may well need some actual maintenance.

Now You See Me, Now You Don't

Some of those attitudes under the surface we are well aware of. Like the person who knows he hates arguments, and consequently avoids confrontation at all costs. Others are more hidden, and are only recognised by the reaction itself. Like the person who finds himself over and over again being "used" in relationships, because he has a hidden fear of rejection, and therefore puts up with what others would never dream of accepting, simply to maintain the relationship. In fact, every attitude implies a consequence.

He Loves Me, He Loves Me Not

Take Sarah. It is a common feeling. Under the surface, she feels that she is not really lovable. She does not like herself over much, and she is never sure if others really like her either. She finds it easier to love, than to accept that anyone else could love *her*. Even someone as affirming and kind as Peter.

Like most people, Sarah is only half aware of the fact although it has been pointed out to her before. Who knows why she is like this? Theories are only ever theories, and one set of circumstances may affect one person one way, and another person in a different way. However, Sarah was deeply upset when her father died, and did miss him so much. She was such a youngster at the time. She needed his presence in her teens – and had this funny feeling of rejection, simply because he was not there.

School was not a happy time either, for the most ridiculous reasons. Girls (like boys!) can be so cruel. Money was short, so Sarah used to have to wear her sister's cast-offs. Unlike the other girls, for many years Sarah never had any new clothes to wear. She didn't really mind, but the other girls used to tease and taunt her, thinking up hurtful nicknames and slogans which they carved into her desk, and chalked up on any available wall space.

What effect did it all have?

Sarah seems to have either persuaded herself or received the impression that there is something unlovely or unlikable about herself. She has carried the thought right into adulthood.

It is very painful to think about. She would certainly never dream of talking about it. As she is more mature now, Sarah suffers much less in company that she used to. She is not nearly so shy as she once was, and has worked hard at "being more outgoing", asking questions and being interested in others and so on.

However, Sarah has married a man who has been divorced. That means he once loved someone else. Someone else shared his bed. His former wife is still alive. He has a son. Of course, Peter is a wonderful husband to Sarah. Yes, he has had this low period recently, but it makes no difference. He is as Christian in his deeds as he is in his words. How could *anyone* doubt him?

Yet Sarah does, irrationally. Not *him* as such. "How can he love *me*? *Does* he really love me? Why *should* he, anyway?" That is what went through Sarah's mind at the end of that conversation about moving. And the issue which set it all off was the thought of moving back to an area which has so many associations with Peter's former marriage. It brought up all the old conflicts in Sarah once again.

It All Depends On Your Foundations

It is a case of every attitude implies a consequence. Sarah's anxiety is to do with the fear lurking beneath the surface – "I'm unlovable, and when someone finds that out they'll reject me." Sarah realises it is irrational to think as she does. But when you see the attitudes beneath, you begin to understand why there is such an unsettling time ahead.

It all depends on your foundations. If the foundations are not sound, you get a shaky building, to say the least. So it is important to make sure that what provides for our potential security and stability under the surface, is in fact properly understood and adequately serviced and provided for.

An Attitude Test

We are going to be looking in a moment with some seriousness at the part our attitudes play in stress and anxiety, and how we can learn to manage them. But first, to start us off, let us think a little more about our own personal attitudes. We need to be aware of their presence in our personalities, and to do some work on trying to *account* for why they are there in the first place.

Here is the exercise, which is to do with our likes and dislikes.

Draw a line down the centre of a page of paper. Head the two columns respectively LIKES/DISLIKES and REASON. Now, under the likes/dislikes column fill in both a like and a dislike reflecting your own feelings, one each for each of these following categories: food, people, places, situations, things. Do not worry if in some categories you *do not* have strong feelings. We are simply trying to get in touch with some of our own basic attitudes. Mark each like with an L and each dislike with a D in brackets.

As this is a private game, you can mention either individual people by name or types if you prefer! It is important to be honest about your feelings. The next stage is to see if you can account for your preferences. Some may be hard or impossible, especially the food, although interestingly someone once said they dislike fish, not because of its flavour or texture, but because of the bones. As a child having his tonsils removed in hospital he had been next to a man who had a fish bone stuck in his throat, and the fear of it had never quite left him! One way or the other, see if you can dig deep down into your attitudes and see how each attitude came to be there in the first place. The food test is simply to get you started.

Give yourself as much time as you need.

By the time you have finished you may be fortunate enough to have learnt something about yourself and about your attitudes which inspire the preferences. You may or may not have realised these before. Of course, some of these attitudes are very everyday, and not at all sinister. But can you see the importance of the principle?

Since anxiety is mainly to do with reactions to our *fears*, and stress to do with our *reaction* to *pressure* occasioned by change – then a primary factor in managing anxiety and stress separately or together, is to tackle these reactions head on. And since reactions are the consequence of attitudes, it is to our attitudes we *must* first go, in order to get to grips with what is motivating and empowering us, sometimes unseen beneath the surface.

Untangling the Knots

All of us are made up of habits, beliefs and attitudes.

Habits are either physical or emotional actions which we

have learned over a long period of time. They take longer to unlearn than learn. But they characterise an important part of what makes us tick as personalities. We have habits of mind, speech and behaviour.

In a sense, a belief is a spoken form of habit. In that I have come to believe something as being habitually true. We always notice our beliefs because we have to *think* about them, albeit briefly, before we say them.

An attitude by contrast is an unspoken belief. Since we do not *think* about the attitude, usually we are not so clearly aware of it. And the attitude comes out instantly as a reaction.

The logic of the attitude is hidden. All that is visible is its required action. Like Sarah's experience:

I have had rejection experiences + rejection experiences are painful = avoid situations with potential for rejection.

Hidden Truths

Two concealed areas to look at, then, are: hidden goals and hidden beliefs.

Hidden goals are important, as we all respond in one way or another to goals which we or others set us. We have been made to achieve. It is the image of God within us. We are creative and energetic.

A HIDDEN GOAL raises the issue: who am I trying to please? Why do I drive myself in this way?

Take George's hidden goal. His mother was very strict and rather stand-offish as a person. George was the youngest of three in his family and positively had to fight for attention.

George's mother's animating concern was that he should do well. Nothing would please her more than to see George stay up late to complete his homework, and subsequently to revise his exams. George learnt then that hard work like nothing else released his mother's affection for him.

We must not make too much of this, but all of us are the products of the influence of our past, even though we may not be entirely bound by it.

Something has to account for this perfectionist trait in George's personality, and the fact that he drives himself so fearfully. Who is he trying to please? If an attitude is an unspoken but learned belief, is it like a habit of mind. George has learned the equation: the harder you work, the more approval you earn. The doctor asked George why he pushed himself so hard. In all honesty, George replied he simply could not help it.

Actually George learnt the ideas as a child from his mother. And ten years after her death, as a mature adult, he is still slave to the same habit of mind: the harder you work, the more approval you receive. Deep down he is still trying to please his mother, and win her approval.

Hidden goals do not always have to be quite so involved. But questions to ourselves such as: "Who am I trying to please? What is my motivation? What do I expect to get out of this?" are instructive. Equally the goals can be negative: "What am I trying to avoid? What am I running away from? What am I afraid of?"

A HIDDEN BELIEF is, of course, similar in that the belief can be a powerful driving force beneath the surface. Sarah's sense of being unlovely is something she has persuaded herself is true. It is a habit of mind.

The vicar had been helpful to Peter when he was talking about unemployment. Peter had pointed out how unsettled he felt. He wanted to feel OK about himself, but could not. The vicar had simply mentioned that it was not Peter's fault he could not get a job. And his question to Peter really set him thinking: "Who told you, you have to be *busy* to be a person?" It was so helpful. It revealed a hidden belief.

With hidden beliefs we have to ask ourselves two things. First, which voice am I listening to? Is it the real me or just buried attitudes from the past? Secondly, did it get the sums right? Has it made $2 + 2 = 5$? In other words, is the belief well founded or not?

Time for an Overhaul

All of us need to overhaul our hidden attitudes, these goals and beliefs. Here is an exercise to help. We are going to have another look at our self-image, and hidden attitudes.

Write down your findings after you have had time to think. First, how do you see yourself? Describe yourself *to* yourself. What do you like? What do you dislike? What would you like to change? Physically, mentally, spiritually or socially.

Second, how do you think others see you? What do you think they like/dislike? How do you think what they see corresponds to what you see?

Third, how would you *like* others to see you, if you could change things?

Now find the pieces of work you did on your fears in Chapter Two, and your stress symptoms and your own stress factors from Chapter Three. Ask yourself if you can account for the reasons why you have those fears, and if they are well founded. Do the sums honestly add up? Or have you made $2 + 2 = 5$?

Can you find any relationship between what you find stressful and your description of yourself, how you are and would like to be? Think about your findings and see what you can learn about yourself.

It may help to write down what you have learnt. And to spend some time praying is the most important part of the exercise. Tell God exactly how you feel about yourself: your fears and concerns, your insecurities and uncertainties. Tell him about your hopes too: the difficulties as well as the joys. Ask him to help you uncover the hidden attitudes, and to find a new freedom within. Here is an outline of a prayer to help, or you can pray silently or in your own words.

"Thank you, Father, that you know me through and through. This is the way I feel about myself. There are things about myself over which I am ashamed. Some things where I am very sensitive. So Father, take these fears and failings, these guiding concerns and attitudes – and bring to me your

healing and your love. I long to know a life of inner freedom,
and I know you can begin to heal and help from this very
moment. I therefore submit what I know of myself to you,
prepared for you to change me. And I willingly offer my
renewed self to you now – to serve you, for your glory. In
Jesus' Name. Amen."

Setting a New Agenda

If you have spent some time pondering and praying, now is
the time for a look at priorities. We have taken a look at the
hidden attitudes, the conflicting voices which prompt us this
way and that. They are like an irritating back-seat driver,
insisting: "Turn here", "Stop there", "Look out!" "Slow
down", "Go faster" and so on. Such voices contribute
significantly to our experience of anxiety and stress. But they
need not be our master.

When we become aware of their covert plans for us, then
not only is forewarned forearmed, but we can, with God's
renewing strength, go to work on them. Usually when we
pray God does not take things away to start off with, though
he is perfectly able to do so. The usual pattern is that he
enables us gradually to cope with the situation in a new way,
so that we ourselves grow in the process, rather than he
simply making life easier for us.

After all we are up against the big question. Who really
does have the deciding say in the unfolding of our futures? If
it is all left to chance, we do have cause to be concerned. But if
God is truly able to direct our lives, then our wisest choice is
to submit ourselves to him.

When Two and Two Make Five!

The move was all right. Not that it was altogether without
incident. Even when you know things are insured, it is heart-
rending to watch a removal man drop a box of china, and then

go and chip your dining-room table. But all that was six months ago, and Sarah, Peter and baby Daniel (who has been growing by leaps and bounds, and is now sleeping through the night) are all very well settled and comfortable together in their little flat.

In fact, the flat is not as small as all that:

"It's just when you have a whole houseful of furniture, it tends to cramp your movements a bit."

Sarah was talking to Peter about the move, and how they had been doing recently. At least they were settled at home. Sarah had been giving Peter a hand with the painting and decorating. It had helped her a great deal, as Peter was particularly appreciative of anything Sarah did.

"Sarah, have I ever told you that I love you?"

"Yes, Peter, many times."

"Well I do . . ."

Sarah felt so glad. Peter was really cherishing her. It was what she longed for, which made what happened the next day all the more painful and surprising.

Peter's mother offered to babysit for Daniel during the lunch hour, so Peter could take Sarah to the supermarket in the car. Peter did not often shop with Sarah, as there was not usually the opportunity. But Peter welcomed the opportunity when it came, even if the supermarket *was* rather busy. He wanted to help Sarah out as much as possible. After all, wives with young babies are stuck indoors for a large part of the day.

"Who is that staring at you, Peter?" Sarah asked. There was a woman in her early forties, looking towards Peter from the fresh meat counter.

Peter began to go red. He hadn't seen Monica for at least five years. Of course, he recognised her at once. He wondered what to do. There was only one thing for it – after all he was a Christian now.

Saying to Sarah under his breath from the corner of his mouth: "It's Monica", and moving quickly towards her, Peter found himself face to face with the woman who walked out on him for another man all those years ago. It seemed like

another world, another age. Instinctively, though, Peter felt
anger welling up inside him, but he checked himself. The
conversation with Monica was civil, even friendly. Peter
looked around for Sarah.

Sarah was nowhere to be seen...

When Peter returned to the multi-storey car park, there she
was, red-eyed, pale, and cross. Very, very cross.

"I just stood there and watched you. Laughing and joking
with that ——. After all she did to you. You were far more
interested in her than me. You didn't once look round to find
me. You don't really love me, do you? It is just words. All you
want is someone to wash your shirts and socks, and make your
bed for you."

And so it went on.

Peter drove Sarah straight back home when she had run out
of energy to say any more. As he travelled back to work in the
car he reflected on how ironic it is that when you try to do the
right thing, you get attacked for it by those who you love
most.

"I'm sorry, Peter," Sarah said, when Peter came through
the door, after work. "I feel better now. I've been having a
think about it. I've been praying too. It is stupid being so
supersensitive. I know you love me. I've been harking back to
the past far too much ..."

Little did Peter understand how destructive Sarah's past
had been to her sense of well-being. It was good she had made
some decisions about herself.

New Directions

It is important to have goals. We talked about some of the
goals we set for ourselves which can be unrealistic or
unhelpful for us. In his letter to the Philippians, Paul talks
about goal-setting in these terms:

"One thing I do: Forgetting what is behind and straining
towards what is ahead, I press on towards the goal to win the
prize for which God has called me heavenwards in Christ
Jesus." Philippians 3:13-14

How embittered and even tormented we can be about the past. Sometimes, it is just the opposite and we can linger over it with nostalgic pleasure: would that we could live it all over again, things are not as they were. Gloating over the past makes us dissatisfied with the present.

Whatever our attitude to the past, one basic truth will help us. The past *is* past. And we should let it be so, not drag it kicking and screaming into the present where it does not belong.

Paul's emphasis is instructive: "Forgetting what is behind". We have to learn to break with the past. Forgetting is a strong word. Paul does not mean a temporary amnesia. The idea is putting something out of mind, refusing to dwell on it any longer, not letting it exert its sway over you. The past is past. So let it be.

This was one of the truths Sarah took hold of. She had heard that passage from the Bible months ago during a radio talk.

It came back to her that afternoon. "It means I really have got to make a break with the past. It is all over. I don't need to keep on feeling fearful about Peter, because of what I persuaded myself was so all those years ago. I am lovable. Peter says so. I must believe him."

That is how Sarah was thinking. As she prayed, so she felt a calm she had not felt for years.

Paul then gives direction:

"Straining towards what is ahead, I press on toward the goal..."

He is saying something about singlemindedness, about giving all your energy to achieve clear goals which are in tune with God's purposes. And there the issue comes into focus.

For Whose Glory?

Have you dealt with your past in the way it needs? Are there still old attitudes and events dogging your present? Will you think of surrendering them to God right now, and ask him to help you break with the past and live now in the present for him?

Because that is in the end the real issue. Whose glory is this all for? It is a profound question, because it is right at the root of the meaning of life itself.

It is perfectly possible to live entirely for my own glory. This world is here to please me. It owes me a living and a favour or two and please me it will.

That, fortunately, is not the way we have been made. Inevitably if we do live that way, after a time we will end up very unhappy, either in this life or when God calls us to account for the way we have lived our lives.

The true way to find liberty is through being prepared to give God the glory. One of the old prayers says: "His service is perfect freedom." And that is true. We are talking about living to please God, putting him first in our lives.

The ancient writer of the Proverbs in the Old Testament says:

"Trust in the Lord with all your heart, and lean not on your own understanding; in all your ways acknowledge him, and he will make your paths straight." Proverbs 3:5–6

That is the way to do it. First at the level of your emotions, "your heart", be prepared to genuinely trust God. Beware of the limitations of the way you see things. "Lean not on your own understanding." God's arithmetic and yours may well be different. He is greater than you, after all.

"In all your ways acknowledge him." That is challenging. It means letting God in, letting him into every detail of your life: into very practical issues like your job and money and so on; into emotional issues like your hopes and fears. If you do that, he pledges himself to guide you. "He will make your paths straight."

We all need new directions, goals which make sense, priorities which glorify God. That is why there is no other way to finally tackle anxiety and stress, unless you see your life, past, present and future, in relation to living for God, living for his glory, living to serve him. It is the attitudes which need to change.

Chapter Five

SOME FALSE PATHS

Often when we are feeling desperate, we will grasp at practically anything. All of us feel the pressures of the world around us, pressures which seem to increase almost visibly, year after year. Hardly surprisingly, there have been many varied and unusual responses to stress and anxiety, both from quasi-religious groups, and from less formal, lifestyle-orientated trends, such as drug-taking and the increased use of alcohol. All of these fringe responses can do far more harm than many of us realise. It is wise to be properly informed, and also warned of what can be false paths. False paths only lead to cul-de-sacs!

It is all in the Mind

Jane was determined to take Saturday afternoon off. There was only one more paper to sit, even though it was a big one. The last six weeks had been so hectic – the play, the end-of-year parties, the argument with her parents over not taking that job in Fleet Street, and then all this revision for finals. It had all been exhausting.

"Excuse me, miss, would you like a free personality test?"

The voice took Jane by surprise. She was lost in her thoughts as she walked down the high street, making for the record shop to buy a new LP.

"I'm sorry," Jane said. "What did you say?"

He was a tall, thin, fair-haired young man. Jane thought he was rather attractive.

"I asked whether you would like a personality test. It is free. It's a service we offer to the public without charge. The test can help you learn more about yourself, help you to overcome your problems, and develop your potential to the full."

Jane was sceptical. But the young man smiled so sweetly. She thought she'd give it a twirl. After all, he'd said it would only take fifteen minutes.

"You sit down here, and you answer these questions about yourself by ticking the box which applies to you. Then when you've finished, we'll plot out your personality on a graph." The young man smiled at Jane again.

When it came to it, Jane was horrified at her personality graph. Someone else, a rather hard-faced girl in her mid-twenties with puffy-looking eyes and a lot of make-up, took Jane through it.

"You're really a depressive personality. Tending towards insecurity, feeling low about your abilities. You're fearful of rejection in relationships, and yes, uncertain too about the future ..."

Jane listened to the catalogue of her alleged inadequacies. Was this the real Jane?

"It must be," she thought. "After all, they said it was scientific."

The young man returned, smiling as he came back into the shop-cum-office. Peering over the graph, he looked suddenly serious.

"I think we may be able to help you, Jane," he said, reading off Jane's name from the top of her answer sheet. "We have a meeting this evening which will introduce you to some principles which will enable you to live a more fulfilled life. It's free. It starts at seven. You will come, Jane, won't you?"

Jane was feeling so tired, and his smile was so winning, she did not have the strength to say no. And anyway, maybe she did need help.

As Jane walked out on to the street, she turned to say goodbye. Her eye caught the bright yellow display of books for sale. "Scientology." That is what it said on the cover. "What on earth," thought Jane, "is Scientology?"

How to Win Friends and Influence People

Amanda, strangely, had a similar experience. Someone had come up to her while she was shopping, and engaged her in conversation. They had said at first they were collecting for missionary work, which had been a big turn-off, for Amanda's father was always going on about giving to missionaries. But the conversation had quickly turned to – where did Amanda reckon she was going in life? It sounded to Amanda just like church. She told them so, only to be informed they were not like other churches, because they believed the Messiah had already returned. And they said they had something new to offer, to help young people to overcome their problems.

Amanda was telling her mother all about the meeting she had been invited to: "They were the friendliest people you could ever wish to meet. We went out to this farm. And we had some food, and then they sang. Then there was a talk. There were several other people who were new like me. They were all so loving. It was ridiculous. Unreal actually. I felt really strange inside. On the one hand, incredibly attracted by their warmth, on the other just plain sceptical about what they were up to. They kind of saturate you with love – and you simply melt. You'll do anything for them after that."

Amanda was waving her arms theatrically in all directions, as she tried to give extra weight to the extraordinary experience she had been through.

Her mother had been listening quietly.

"Did they tell you what they call themselves, Amanda?"

"They don't make a secret of it. But they don't exactly spell it out unless you ask them. I saw the words 'Holy Spirit Association' on their missionary leaflet, and also 'Movement for the Unification of world wide Christianity'. It didn't click at first. Then I asked one of the Swedish boys at the farm if he was a Moonie. He didn't seem to like the name. But it was he who used the title, the Unification Church ..."

The False Way of the Cults

Many of the cults offer new, more fulfilled ways of living. Freedom from anxiety and stress is one of the many promises they make; which is why it is important to be clear about what they really stand for. They claim to be in touch with God. And of course they reckon their way of doing things is the *only* way – because it is newly revealed, and supersedes all previous models!

But what actually *is* a cult?

The word "cult" is used pretty loosely these days. It usually refers to some kind of religion or religious group. In the past the word has been used more specifically for something definitely related in some way to Christianity, but a distortion of it. Many of the cults, or sects, as they are also known, have this relationship. Jehovah's Witnesses, Mormons, Moonies, Children of God all share something in common with Christianity. Though their teaching is a horrendous *distortion* of the Christian gospel. But today we can also include under the heading of "cults" such varied groups as Hare Krishna, Scientology, Divine Light Mission and so on. These groups often owe the origins of their thinking to the East, though not necessarily. All of them have a "religious" intention. They offer special rewards to the initiated, often in terms of self-actualisation, fulfilment and freedom from pressures – like anxiety and stress.

When is a Cult not a Cult?

It is important to know what we are dealing with when confronted by the claims of a cult. Basically, any claim which does not recognise the overall authority of Jesus, the

Lordship of Christ, is either sub-Christian or not Christian at all.

The Apostle Paul helps us when he says:

"If you confess with your mouth, 'Jesus is Lord', and believe in your heart that God raised him from the dead, you will be saved." Romans 10:9

Paul is linking the claim to follow Jesus and be under his authority and mastery ("Jesus is Lord") with the historical facts of the gospel ("God raised him from the dead"). Any attempt to divorce the figure of Jesus from the historical Jesus who was born, lived and died in Palestine, whose life, deeds and sayings the gospels record, is less than Biblical historical Christianity, and therefore a distortion of the truth. Many of the sects can be seen to be wayward at this point. They present an emaciated Jesus, not fully man and fully God as the Scriptures record him to be. ("And The Word was made flesh, and dwelt among us ... full of grace and truth." John 1:14, AV) Not only do these sects have a reduced *view* of Jesus, they have also reduced his *role* for him.

Some Biblical Norms

Just as it is a good test of the health of any Christian or Christian fellowship to ask Is there a genuine love for Jesus, are they Christ-centred? So it is a way of seeing whether the claims of any group are centrally Christian or whether they have distorted the truth and become a cult. Are they really Christ-centred? Are they working for his glory, seeking to serve him?

Paul says:

"God ... gave him the name which is above every name, that at the name of Jesus every knee should bow ... and every tongue confess that Jesus Christ is Lord, to the glory of God the Father." Philippians 2:9–11 (NIV)

So who is getting the honour? Who is it all centred on? Christ or who else? It is an important question to ask. Many cults have some other figure or concern at the centre of their actual activity and thinking.

Then there is the question of the message itself. The Apostle Peter says: "Christ died for sins once for all, the righteous for the unrighteous, to bring you to God." 1 Peter 3:18

Here is the central message of the Good News about Jesus. He died as a sacrificial substitute for us, to pay the fine for our sins. And as the Saviour he is able to offer us complete forgiveness and a new start with God now, because his death has paid the price we could not pay for ourselves.

The cults have little understanding of the seriousness of sin, or this offer of complete forgiveness by Jesus – based on his sacrificial death and resurrection. Yet this is the central message of the whole Bible.

So here are three basic tests of the irreducible minimum for claims to Christian belief. Do they have a full view of Jesus, holding his divinity and manhood together? Are they genuinely Christ-centred and seeking to live for his glory? And do they really grasp the promise of the gospel: the *free* forgiveness of Jesus as the only way to come to know God?

There is much more to Christianity than that, but the cults invariably diverge at one of these points. They are the truth-distorters. They take their authority from some "inspired" writing, which in practice is either regarded as the authoritative interpretation of the Bible (like "Science and Health with Key to the Scriptures" of the Christian Scientists) or as superseding it entirely (like the Divine Principle of the Unification Church). Most cults have some written authoritative book or books, even, in the case of the Jehovah's Witnesses, their own weird and messed-about translation of the Bible, which has been made to say the things they want it to say! Spiritual help is no use to us if it is bogus.

Promises, Promises

There are many promises in the Bible, some of which we have looked at already, which have profound things to say about our emotional health, and the way we handle pressures in our lives. But the promises made by some of the cults are unhealthy. They neglect the reality of God's love and grace and quite often substitute some form of quasi-brainwashing technique to help you to *feel* better – though do not change any of your painful basic *attitudes*, or stressful *lifestyle*.

The higher thinking of the Christian Scientists is a useful example. Christian Scientists, taking their cue from their founder Mary Baker Eddy, do not believe, according at least to their literature, that there is any such thing as objective illness or pain. It is an illusion. So you must simply "up" your thinking and pretend or persuade yourself it isn't there. It is a very eastern way of thinking – and divorced from reality. Yet it is surprising how many people are still influenced by such ideas.

Only Jesus lets us be fully realistic about ourselves. He insists we face the hurdles and not run away. I heard of a millionaire who, having built himself a golf course in the United States, was having trouble with the bunker on the fourteenth hole. Every time he faced the fourteenth, he found himself stuck inconveniently in the bunker for several shots. One day, being a millionaire, he decided to have the bunker removed. It certainly made his game easier, but it didn't turn him into a better golfer!

God could remove the bunkers in our lives if he wanted to. But he does not. Because facing the bunkers often helps us to grow and become mature. Jesus doesn't offer any form of escapism. He only offers involvement. He asks us to face ourselves and our challenges, and then gives us strength and direction to cope. His promises are very different from the cults'. They are realistic. They deal with the underlying problems. They don't evade the issue. Beware the false way of the cults.

Seeking to Compensate

Of course, there are other ways we seek to compensate when

the pressure hots up. Some people wouldn't recognise a cult if they saw one – but they are much more familiar with the more civilised compensations, those compensations sometimes politely called indulgences.

... Helps you Work, Rest and Play

George sank into his chair. At least the train had been on time. But what a Monday.

"It's all very well for the senior partner to return in glory and start ordering everyone about again. But someone has been covering all his work for the last five weeks. It is not particularly pleasant, when he starts changing all the procedures you have been busily setting up for him in his absence, and throwing everyone into confusion into the bargain."

"Don't worry about that now, George dear, have a cup of tea and relax. We can talk about it later when you've had a bit of a rest."

Mary turned to put the kettle on. As she went over to the sink George stopped her.

"Not for me, Mary."

"Oh. Aren't you thirsty?"

"I'd rather have something stronger."

Mary thought that was unlike George. George is a creature of habit, and he always has his cup of tea when he comes in after work.

Opening the cupboard, Mary was surprised to find the bottle of whisky she had bought last week was already two thirds empty. It surely could not have been Ben or Amanda. No possibility. They would not like the taste. So that's what she'd been smelling on his breath recently. Handing the glass to George, Mary decided to say nothing more than:

"Here you are, dear."

A Little of what you Fancy

Peter still wasn't used to selling cars. He had found these early months predictably stressful. Still, there were compensations – like the local. When he went to the pub at lunchtime with his father, it was not so much the beer which provided the attraction, more the cold buffet.

"You've put on some weight recently, haven't you, Peter?" his father said. "You look a little more human now. Thought you were going to fade away."

Peter laughed.

"It's nice to see you looking a little more healthy, Peter. Right now, what's it going to be today. The chicken pie with potato salad? Or the cold meats with tomato and chips? You have to wait five minutes for the chips."

"I'll wait for the cold meats," Peter said. Then he added: "Can you get me some french bread and butter while I'm waiting?"

The apple pie and cream was delicious too. On the way out Peter bought some chocolate to nibble at through the afternoon. It made him feel so much better, took his mind off things somehow.

"Darling, you are getting fat." Peter was bending over to find himself something to eat from the refrigerator. Sarah had noticed his increasingly bulging waist-line. "You can't be hungry at nine thirty in the evening. We only finished supper at seven thirty."

Peter tried not to be cross. Somehow he realised he had got himself into the habit of eating for the sake of eating, or rather, when he was honest about it, eating to compensate when he was feeling worried or tensed up.

"I'm only going to have a little more of the pie, Sarah."

The grim thought of heart attacks filled Sarah with dread. The effect of these little indulgences was beginning to show.

We have to watch ourselves. We are all prone to indulging ourselves to compensate for anxiety and stress. The danger is we mask our feelings, which are the indicators that something is wrong, by taking our mind off the issue with the pleasant diversion of the indulgence. But there are two consequences. One, we fail to deal with the issue underlying the feelings.

We, in effect, try to run away or escape from the perhaps painful conclusion that we have to do something about it. Second, the indulgence in itself can become harmful. Like a drug, we become hooked on it. It is the "fix" which works just nicely to enable us to cope with the unpleasant feelings engendered by stress and anxiety.

Such addictions have their unfortunate spin-offs. Of course, there is nothing wrong with food and alcohol in themselves. But go beyond the point of moderation and you run risks. You do not have to be very overweight to be obese. And that does run risks, risks to your health in all kinds of ways: heart disease, high blood pressure and other degencrative conditions. Alcohol can similarly be detrimental if taken too much and too frequently. People in stressful occupations are particularly at risk from alcoholism. And it can happen to the most intelligent, well-informed people. No one is necessarily immune. Doctors themselves account for a very high percentage of those who suffer from alcoholism.

So a little of what you fancy is only going to do you good if it *is* a little. Otherwise for work, rest and play it is better to face the issues before you, than simply trying to escape. Which brings us to another form of escapism.

The Confusions of the Mystics

Jane had decided that Scientology was definitely not for her. All those weird types. Their eyes seemed so glazed . . .

Penny had suggested that Jane go along to the relaxation class that John Cameron, the producer of the play Jane had been in, himself attended.

"They say it is really relaxing, Jane." Penny wanted to persuade Jane to go. Jane had been so uptight recently, it was obvious she needed some help.

"You are right, Penny, it is the one thing I cannot do at the moment. Relaxation is just what I need. I'll phone up John, and find out when he is going next."

In fact the relaxation sessions turned out to be a yoga class.

It *was* relaxing, despite the contortions! Yoga turned out to be fun. However, as the weeks went by, Jane became increasingly anxious about the philosophy of it all. She was no fool. All this stuff about emptying your mind. As far as Jane was concerned, that was all very well, but all the old garbage came floating back once you were upright again. After all, it belongs there!

John laughed, as Jane explained her views over her cup of herbal tea. They were really into macrobiotics.

"I don't think you've quite grasped it, Jane. The philosophy of the East is that our concerns and pressures are mere illusions. We must empty ourselves of all that is not of the spirit. That is why I meditate every day. I concentrate on a sound and seek to empty myself of every material thought, even thoughts about myself. I try to give myself up to the total reality of all things, and perceive myself as simply part of the whole."

"Is that why you've had your hair cut so short?" Jane could be cynical when she wanted to.

John did not react visibly. He tried to regard his hurt reaction as illusory and unreal. Repressing his feelings, he smiled at Jane. Somehow though, he could not help himself thinking how self-opinionated she was.

What do we Make of It?

The difficulty with *all* these issues is that they inevitably contain a grain of truth. Yet at the same time there are elements which are either "way out" or simply not true at all. And they affect the way we cope with anxiety and stress. It is no good running away. Running away is no solution. You have to face the issues. Meditation therefore has its dangers because, again, it is an evasion. It helps you *feel* better, temporarily, but offers you nothing in return to help you face the situation of discontent. It is positively harmful when it speaks of self-emptying. The weak parts of our personalities do need to be dealt with. But that is a far cry from emptying ourselves of our personality altogether.

The Bible speaks of meditation in several different ways. But, by contrast, meditation in the Bible always has an *object*, something to meditate upon, something which will improve us if we learn from it.

So the Old Testament character Joshua is told to meditate on God's word day and night. He is then given the challenge to put what he learns into practice. After that comes the promise: "Then you will be prosperous and successful ... Be strong and courageous. Do not be terrified; do not be discouraged, for the Lord your God will be with you wherever you go." Joshua 1:8-9

For us, this is not a formula for instant solutions to our problems. As Jesus implied, when he told us to take up our cross, being a Christian can mean we sometimes face particularly difficult times in our lives. Yet we can be assured, amidst these difficulties, that same strength, courage and guidance from God, promised to Joshua, will be ours daily as we meditate deeply upon God's word. This is the essence of Biblical meditation.

Then there is this element of stillness, which is so attractive for those with a taste for meditation, Yoga or TM. The Psalmist's words, "Be still, and know that I am God" (Psalm 46:10), show us several truths, and put the concept of stillness into focus.

The expression "be still" in Hebrew literally means "shut up and stop what you are doing." That is telling us something about our hectic lifestyle. We do need to stop, stop thinking, talking and doing, and know, know deep down in all the richness of his reality, that God is God. This is the way to grow through Biblical meditation. It is helpful to begin a time when you read the Bible and pray, by concentrating silently on one single truth about God: his love, or holiness; his sovereignty or power; his mercy or justice. It is true what they say: "The things of earth grow strangely dim in the light of his glory and grace."

Just what the Doctor Ordered?

There are still other false paths to avoid. Some have value on the surface, but deep down lack substance, because they fail to help us face the underlying factors. Positive thinking, relaxation techniques and self-hypnosis are all of this order.

The increasing lobby for the legalisation of cannabis in the UK is further evidence of the escapist mentality. Its great danger is not only that it leads on to harder drugs, but it encourages drug-taking as an escape from facing facts.

At a more respectable level, whilst tranquillisers and antidepressants are a wonderful gift from God to us in the latter part of the twentieth century, when prescribed appropriately and wisely, the simple truth is that many people are just as hooked on medication which is singularly inappropriate for their needs, because an overworked doctor did not have time to talk through adequately the problems his patient was facing.

Of course, this medicine is very often necessary and extremely valuable. Sadly many simply run for the bottle, rather than face the fact that they must tame their rebel emotions, and learn to manage their reactions.

The Plain Truth

The plain truth is this! There is no substitute for courage in facing our true selves. There is no easy way of escape. False paths are false friends. They betray us in the end, which only compounds our problems, as sadly so many have found to their cost.

Chapter Six

FINDING FREEDOM

In a world of pressures, where personal anxiety and the experience of stress abound, how is it possible to find freedom? Real freedom from the painful impact of those issues in life which tend to knock us about, and give us so much discomfort and dissatisfaction about living? Jesus once said: "You will know the truth and the truth will set you free." John 8:32

It is time to look in more detail at the freedom Jesus brings. And how the truth he makes known can bring liberty to our lives, particularly in those areas of anxiety and stress. As Jesus says later in the same passage: "If the Son sets you free, you will be free indeed." John 8:36

The Long Search

"If only I had faith."

There was silence as the student counsellor considered what Jane had said. "You mean that there's something you'd like to believe in?"

"Yes," said Jane. "I'm so worried about the future. I wish I knew whether there is a God who cares. Who knows my future and can guide me. I suppose it is just wishful thinking."

Again the counsellor paused. Was Jane going to add to what she had said? After a few moments, the counsellor asked Jane:

"Are you worried about what is going to happen after your results come out? About how the future is going to unfold for you?"

"Am I worried?" Jane expostulated. "Of course I'm worried. I wouldn't be here if I wasn't worried."

Tears welled up in Jane's eyes. She held back for a moment to compose herself. But she couldn't help choking out the words:

"I think I've blown it. I've probably flunked my exams. And I've chucked up the offer of a perfectly good job. My parents aren't prepared to help because they are angry at me for what I've done. I've really blown it this time. And I don't know what I'm going to do."

Jane began to cry. She was a little embarrassed at crying in front of someone she had only just met. But out came the tears nonetheless.

After some minutes, when she felt a little better, Jane said:

"I'm serious. I really do wish I had faith. I've noticed some of my friends who are Christians seem to manage much better than me. Not all of them. But I have this friend called Penny who goes to church. And she is really together. You know, the silly thing is, I haven't even a clue where to start. I've tried dabbling with one or two things here and there, but without much success. I don't know what to do. I'm in a mess."

The counsellor nodded understandingly. "Have you thought of asking Penny about it?" It was a helpful suggestion, much more helpful than his initial suggestion for Jane to see the chaplain, because Jane is rather suspicious of authority figures at the moment.

As she left the student health centre, Jane made a mental agreement with herself to see Penny soon and have a thoroughly good chat about things. For all the embarrassment, it has been worth seeing the counsellor after all.

That Morning After Feeling

Many of us have woken up one grey morning to find our lives and ourselves in a proper muddle. We do not know which way to turn. We are subject to all the vicious pressures of existence. And when something difficult comes along, it is the straw which sits too heavily on the camel's back!

Jesus himself lived in the same kind of world as us. He was subject to enormous pressures: other people's expectations; opposition which grew into a bitter hatred; the desertion of his friends; the pressures of people clamouring for his attention; having to be a public figure and cope with the glare of publicity; and finally, to face betrayal, torture, and a horrifyingly cruel and painful criminal's death. So when Jesus talks about freedom, it is not glib. We can be absolutely sure he knows about the pressures we are under, and, even more importantly, just what it is which really enslaves us.

A Room with a View

Penny couldn't have been more delighted. When Jane phoned up a couple of days after her meeting with the counsellor, Penny had been able to suggest that Jane come up to her room that very afternoon. And the idea that after some tea and chat, they should both go out together to see that new film which had swept the board at the Oscars ceremony last week, was a real help too.

"Oh Penny, everything has gone wrong for me recently. It's like a house beginning to slowly crumble to pieces. It's awful, I feel as though I can't get out, that I'm trapped – that it is all going to come down on top of me."

"Tell me more of what you said on the phone," Penny urged. "You said you'd told the counsellor at the health centre that you really wish you could believe, or words to that effect. And he said you should think about talking to a Christian friend about it."

"Yes," said Jane. "It has been on my mind for some time. I want to have faith like you, Penny. I'm worried about the future. I need something to lean on. It's even more than that. I need to know the truth. And I've noticed something attractive in the Christians I've met. It is something I don't have. A kind of peace or something . . . If there is one thing I lack at the moment, it's peace all right."

Jane went on to tell Penny in more detail what had been going on in her mind over these past weeks, how she had been feeling, and how she had been rushing around like a mad thing. Penny listened carefully, and after a while asked Jane whether she would like to have a look at a Bible to check out what Jesus says about some of the issues they'd been talking about. Jane agreed, and they turned up first of all that comment of Jesus' in John's gospel:

"Then you will know the truth, and the truth will set you free." John 8:32

Of course, literature is Jane's subject, so she immediately wanted to read round the comment to see the context of what Jesus is saying.

"Actually, Penny, those words follow on from the previous verse," Jane said, with all the enthusiasm of discovery.

"In verse 31 Jesus says: 'If you hold to my teaching, you are really my disciples. Then you will know the truth and the truth will set you free.'"

It was an entirely new view for Jane.

"So I see now, it is a matter of putting into practice Jesus' teaching, that shows you to be a real follower of Jesus himself. Then you begin to know freedom."

Jane's approach was thoughtful. It is so important to see these things in context. But Penny wanted to point out the wider context to Jane to complete the picture.

Jane had been saying earlier that she had always tried to follow the ten commandments. She was not perfect, but she was not that bad either! So they had a look together at what Jesus considers the most important of all the commandments, and what is therefore the foundation of his teaching, which he has been referring to in the verses they had just been looking at.

In Mark 12:28–31, Jesus is asked what he considers of all the commandments is in fact the most important. Jesus replies:

"The most important one is ... 'Love the Lord your God with all your heart and with all your soul and with all your mind and with all your strength.' The second is this: 'Love your neighbour as yourself.' There is no commandment greater than these."

Jane grinned.

"The second's easier than the first, isn't it? Though I'm not sure that even the second is that easy when you think about it. Honestly, Penny, I'm a non-starter on the first. Love the Lord your God! God has never even had a look in on my life. Up to now I have been going my own sweet way. Religion has bored me silly. And I used to think Christians were wets. I think I'm beginning to see things differently now ..."

There was a long silence as Jane looked down again at Jesus' words. She was very thoughtful for a while.

"The counsellor initially suggested I go to speak to the chaplain. I didn't like the idea particularly. I prefer your chocolate biscuits, Penny!" Penny laughed. "But I thought I'd sit in at the back of the service in chapel this morning and have a listen to what he had to say. He was quite good. One thing he said has just come back to me. 'Sin is breaking God's laws. But the number one sin as far as God is concerned is simply shutting him out of your life.' I think I can see now where he got that from."

There was a pause, as again Jane seemed to be composing her thoughts. "That's me, isn't it? I've been running the show, sitting there in the front seat. I've done it my way. And that's why. That's why it's all tumbling down on me!"

It was quite a realisation, and Jane knew it. Just as she said it, the alarm on her watch went off. They both looked up and smiled. It was time for the film. She and Penny had been talking solidly for the last three hours. They would talk again. Jane wanted to.

The Buck Stops Here

The first stage in becoming a Christian is to *admit your need*.

Unless we admit that we need God's help, he can do nothing for us. We have to admit morally that we have sinned. That means we have broken God's laws, and most of all we have not let him be in charge of our lives. It means admitting therefore that we have been in the wrong, and we need beyond everything his forgiveness and love.

The Apostle Paul spells all this out in Romans 3:23: "*Everyone* has sinned and is far away from God's saving presence" (Good News Bible). We are all in the same boat, there is no one who can claim immunity. We have all sinned. It is an unpopular word, but a universal fact.

However, there is more to it than that. Paul continues in the very next verse, verse 24: "But by the free gift of God's grace all are put right with him through Jesus Christ, who sets them free."

So here is our next step. Having *admitted* our need, we must next *believe* not only is Jesus the Son of God, but that his death on the cross is God's way of making the payment for our sins which we are unable to pay for ourselves. We are therefore offered forgiveness. And of course no one can be fully forgiven unless they are prepared to receive that forgiveness and live differently from now on, so a change of mind *and* behaviour is called for. The forgiveness is free, but it must be valued.

Who Decides on these Oscars, Anyway?

Jane and Penny pushed their way through the crowd. Everyone seemed to have enjoyed it. People were talking at the top of their voices. A hamburger and a Coke were definitely called for.

Maybe it was because it was so late that the hamburger place was only half full. It had been a particularly long film. There was a table in the corner at which Jane sat down, while Penny went and procured the refreshments ...

As Jane sat there her mind went back to their afternoon's discussion.

"Do I need to make any changes in my life? It is quite a big thing becoming a Christian."

Jane began to feel fearful.

"What if it is all just a sell out? A put-up job? Perhaps it is all just rubbish?"

Penny appeared with two hamburgers, two Cokes, paper napkins and extra ketchup. Jane munched her way through the first bite.

"I reckon the play was miles better. I mean it was a good film, but so commercial. The play was subtle – it left something to your imagination."

They'd done the play at college in Jane's first year. Both she and Penny had played small parts. Jane had found going to see the film quite therapeutic.

"I don't know who chooses these Oscar Awards anyway," said Penny. "But you must admit technically it was brilliant. Fabulous photography and sound. And the acting in its way was pretty good."

Jane reluctantly agreed. Suddenly she changed the subject. It had been on her mind all evening.

"Penny, how do I go about becoming a Christian?"

Penny had just taken an enormous bite of hamburger and made appropriate noises! It gave her time to think of the best way of helping Jane.

"I think, Jane, there is something you have to consider. If you want to become a Christian, which means in practice becoming a follower of Jesus yourself, it will mean making changes in your life. It means being prepared to turn over your life *completely* to God. And that implies being genuinely sorry for everything that has been wrong, and deciding to break with any wrong practice you've been involved in. That is what the Bible means by repentance."

Jane listened carefully, while Penny continued.

"It will mean being prepared to be a Christian in all situations. At home, in the college, when you eventually start working. It means letting Christ influence your relationships, your values, your hopes and fears. It means believing that

Jesus died for you, that he loves you. And asking him into your life."

"That is really what I want, Penny." Jane's tears were a mixture of sorrow – for some reason she could clearly see now how she had been in the wrong – and of joy – there is a way forward; and there is a promise of freedom.

Though it was late, the two girls went back to Penny's room for coffee. Penny prayed with Jane. And Jane asked Jesus to come personally into her life. She asked his forgiveness. And she resolved to follow him for ever. It was the beginning of a brand new life for Jane. The truth that sets you free.

Finding Freedom

The steps Jane took are the steps we must all take, if we wish to find the freedom God longs for us to have. After all, coming to know him is only the initial stage in a longer process of restoration he wishes to work in our personalities. Perhaps it would be useful to briefly go over the steps again which enable us to become Christians. They are a simple ABCD.

A: something to ADMIT. The first step is to recognise your need, and admit morally that you have sinned, that you do need God's forgiveness. You have been in the wrong, and you need his forgiveness and love.

B: something to BELIEVE. The second step is to believe that Jesus is not only the Son of God, but that he died on the cross so your sins can be forgiven. This is the hub of the matter. Jesus' resurrection guarantees the claim that Jesus is who he says he is, the Son of God, and that he has dealt effectively with our sins by his death – and so we are offered freely in consequence forgiveness and a new start in life.

C: something to CONSIDER. It is important to consider that Jesus makes demands as well as offers. It will mean turning away from everything you know to be wrong – and accepting his mastery over every aspect of your life. It will mean joining a church, as all Christians will now be your brothers and sisters. God does not want us to be Christians without going to church on Sundays. Worship and Christian friendship as well as contributing your abilities in Christian service are important parts of the package. It is important of course to choose a live church, where the teaching is Biblical, and the worship alive. It will mean being a Christian in all areas of life, with no exceptions, and going back on ways which are wrong.

D: something to DO. In the end it has to become personal. There is something for you to do, and something which God will do. On your part there has to be a decision now to make this commitment, if you have never made it before. If you are not sure about where you stand with God you can always ink in, what previously you may only have put in pencil. On God's part, if you make this commitment, he will forgive you totally everything that has been wrong in your life: thoughts and actions, past, present and future. And more than that, at the moment you make that commitment to him through prayer, he will bring in the Holy Spirit, who is God himself in all his power and strength, right into the centre of your life: to empower and strengthen you and enable you to follow Jesus in God's enabling way, both now and forever. It is forever, because he will give you the gift of eternal life. It is a wonderful promise.

A Prayer for Commitment

This is a prayer you might use to come to God in this way. You can put it into your own words, or use it as it is written. The important thing is to be sincere, and believe because of Jesus' death and resurrection, God will hear you and answer you. You may like to read over those three passages, Mark 12:28–31, John 8:31–32 and Romans 3:23,24, to remind yourself of the truths which undergird these thoughts. Here is the prayer:

"Heavenly Father, I admit that it is true – I have sinned. I am sorry for what I have done to hurt you and other people. And thank you that I can come to you through Jesus Christ, that he is the only one to turn to. Now, as far as I am able, Lord, I turn away from everything I know to be wrong. I seek your full forgiveness and pardon. Thank you for Jesus, that he died for me, that he rose from the dead, that he is alive.

"I therefore take his promised gift of new life and the peace which he brings. Thank you for the Holy Spirit which you have now given me. Thank you that you have given me a new family in the church, and all Christians everywhere are my brothers and sisters in Christ. I pray and thank you in Jesus' name. Amen."

You cannot be a private Christian! Take a hot coal out of a fire, and it soon will lose its glow and die. It is important for us all to have the strength and encouragement of Christian friends. So, if you have sincerely prayed that prayer to God, you are now a Christian. It is the best thing you have ever done in your life. Do aim to make contact with other Christians as soon as you can. And tell someone today what you have done. It will help you to come out, and be openly recognised as a follower of Jesus Christ.

The Road Ahead

A new relationship with God through Jesus Christ opens up so many possibilities as far as the road ahead is concerned. The discomforts we suffer because of those situations which give rise to unpleasant feelings within, can be handled in a vastly different way. Guilt, uncertainty, disappointment, failure, rejection are all painful experiences. Knowledge of some of the major Biblical truths about God enable us to cope in a new way with these stress or anxiety-making factors. This is what Jesus means about knowing the truth, and the freedom that the truth brings.

God Rules OK

Jane has been a Christian now for six weeks. Penny has

continued to be helpful, meeting Jane for Bible study and prayer and general encouragement. Their friendship has grown much deeper. And Jane has been brave about sharing her faith, yet in a natural and unaffected way.

Jane's results were disappointing. She only just passed. But that was better than failing! It used to be that other people expected Jane to be super-brilliant, but she was beginning to realise other people's expectations really do not matter so much. It was, in any case, the best she could have hoped for under the circumstances. The major difference was she no longer felt paralysed with anxiety about the future.

"You know, Penny, I went through agonies of uncertainty about the future. I think I've learnt what it means when the Bible says, 'perfect love casts out fear'. In that I realise God does love me perfectly, and he's not going to let me fall into the drink. So I may as well trust him to guide me and see me through."

Guide Me, O Thou Great Redeemer – Facing Uncertainty

One of the great truths of the whole Bible is that God is able to guide his people in all circumstances. The limiting factor is *us* – when we are not willing to let him guide us! A great deal of our anxiety stems from uncertainty about the future.

"How will things turn out?"

"Will I manage?"

"Will it be all right?"

It is humanly a struggle for us to let God be God, and hand over our futures to him. Of course, that is not meant to be a recipe for doing nothing, as though we should expect God to do it all. But if we are prepared to trust God with our futures, he has promised to guide us.

Why do we find all this such a struggle? Everybody prefers certainty to uncertainty. But then if the world were one great long certainty from beginning to end, it would be a very boring place. There would be no surprises, nothing to look forward to – and no need of God. God wants us to learn to trust him. That strangely, is one of the reasons we have uncertainty. It has an educative function. Paul explains the principle when he says:

"We live by faith, not by sight." (2 Cor. 5:7)

It is one of our Creator's educative disciplines for us.

Faith is a kind of decision. It does not matter if you can not *feel* you trust God. After all, our feelings, though important, are a notoriously unreliable guide to reality. Faith means the decision to believe God is there in control, and to give up fussing, and accept that he will guide – and is working things out for the best possible outcome in his grand scheme of things. So when your feelings bob up and tell you: "It is all going to be terrible, you'll never cope", turn back to them and say: "I'm not going to listen to you any more. You've been made redundant. I've decided to believe what God says from now on!"

Do not risk your future to your feelings. Feelings need to learn to follow the facts, not the other way round. It is the best way to deal with uncertainty. By facing it!

If only they knew – Facing Guilt

Another issue which causes us a great deal of stress and anxiety symptoms is guilt. We all tend to bury those things we are ashamed of. Skeletons in the cupboard are a much more common reality than most people suppose. The way to deal with guilt is to be realistic about it, not bury it. Admit it to yourself and to God. You see, the worst things about yourself God already knows about. Maybe you cannot stand yourself for letting yourself do that thing, or say those words, or agree to that action. God knows all about it. He paid the price for the worst you ever did or ever will do, however horrible, by Jesus' death. He wants you to know that forgiveness. Not to let that guilt dog you from now to your dying day. How will you ever be effective as a person, if you are spending half your energy trying to hide part of yourself and your past from others, as well as from your own conscious mind?

"If anybody does sin, we have one who speaks to the Father in our defence – Jesus Christ, the Righteous One. He is the atoning sacrifice for our sins." (1 John 2:1–2)

Those words were written to Christians. All of us sin in our adult Christian lives. It does not mean though, either that we should lean back on easy forgiveness, or behave by contrast as though we are so terrible we can never be forgiven. It is a kind of blasphemy to suggest that God is not capable of forgiving what I have done. And do not forget, once confessed, a sin is done with. No fishing. No gloating. No going back.

Should sin or guilt be confessed to someone else?

Sometimes it is helpful to unburden to a Christian friend or a minister. It is helpful to have them pray with you and assure you from the Bible of God's forgiveness. But here is a useful principle. Private sin should be confessed privately. Personal sins – involving someone else – should, where appropriate, be confessed personally. Only public sins should be confessed publicly. The whole world does not need to know about your wrong thoughts. If you have actually hurt someone terribly, then go and say sorry. If you have harmed some public group by some thoughtless or wrong action, say so publicly. The world does need to see in our day and age people who admit with dignity both their accountability and responsibilities. And when you have done it, you have done it. If God says you are forgiven, you had better believe it. Don't try and atone for your sins yourself. Jesus has done it – he doesn't require any contribution from you!

Feeling Let Down – Facing Disappointment and Failure

Jane's initial reaction to the news of her finals was real disappointment. She did not expect to do well. But she expected to do better than just pass . . .

George was terribly worried about Amanda's boyfriend. He

was considerably older than her. George told Amanda to be careful. He felt such a failure when Mary told him Amanda was on the pill . . .

When Peter had lost his job at the bakery, of course it was not his fault. He could not help feeling a failure though. Every time they told him there was nothing for him, when he used to go down to the job centre, it seemed only to rub in the horrid truth . . .

Failure and disappointment are part of life. We all have certain kinds of expectations for ourselves and others. And when those expectations are violated, the "down" of failure and disappointment are what we feel. However, some of us are prone to let these temporary feelings take up a permanent home in the residence of our thought world. We become permanently disappointed; or permanent failures; or afraid that we might be.

We then find that anything which may add to our sense of failure is so painful that we avoid such situations like the plague. Our disappointment turns to a bitter outlook on life, causing us a certain kind of stress. We refuse to respond positively, and therefore fail to derive benefit from the relaxation and recreation which might otherwise be ours – so continuously unsettled do we feel. So what if we have failed! Jesus specialises in failures in that he sees everyone has sinned, broken and marred their relationship with God. Who then is making the standards? When we become Christians we are no longer failures, we are restored. We belong to God. We are loved. And there is purpose in our lives. Disappointments there may well be still – but their effect must not be allowed to be permanent. One word accounts for all this. It is the word "acceptance".

We have to learn to accept that God forgives failure, and restores the lives of the disappointed. Someone as important as David, King of Israel, was a terrible failure. Morally he was really a failure, by his adultery with Bathsheba, yet God restored him. The Apostle Peter actually denied Jesus, not once, but three times. Yet Jesus restored him.

What good would it have been if David or Peter or many other Biblical characters had kept their heads in their hands for the rest of their lives and bewailed their stupidity or ill fortune? God restores. And we must accept that he *has* restored us and *will* restore us. Facing it is the best way to deal with disappointment and failure – because they are the dangerous building blocks of stress and anxiety.

No one Loves me any more – Facing Rejection

Sarah's great problem was with rejection. She had been fearful of relationships ever since she was in her teens.

Rejection is again something many people fear. To an extent, of course, it is a natural reaction. But it can get beyond reasonable limits, and become a cause of anxiety and stress-related symptoms. What can be done to help?

It may be useful to realise that Jesus knew the experience of rejection intimately. It was prophesied that he would be "despised and rejected by men" (Isaiah 53:3). And the experience of his life confirmed the validity of that prophetic statement. It helps to know that when we tell God about such fears we do have, we can know that he understands completely. Jesus has been through himself what we fear most. It is important to realise he has been through the worst we could ever face. And that is why we know he understands.

But above all, what will help us most in dealing with the fear of rejection is to know that God *accepts* us. He knows everything about us. All the bits we don't like, or are ashamed of, or would like to change and cannot. He knows us, loves us and has made us his children. He has made you his child.

It is good to savour the truth: I am really accepted and loved by God. "Ransomed, healed, restored, forgiven." Try beginning each day, as you wake up, by saying to yourself: "I *am* accepted." Think about it consciously, then thank God that it is true. If God accepts you thoroughly, knowing you as you really are, does it really matter what others think? Why do you live your life worrying what other people might or do think about you? Dwell on this great thought: "How great is the love the Father has lavished on us, that we should be called children of God!" (1 John 3:1). That truth, when you really make it your own, meditating on it regularly, is a real restorer of perspectives, and a banisher of fears. It helps just as much as when we are tempted to consistently compare ourselves with others. Be like yourself, not someone else! God has made you special. Do believe it. You are accepted. You have much to offer in your own right.

Setting your Sights High – Facing the Truth

What is meant by the sufficiency of God?

It really means seeing just how big God is. That he is sufficient to every circumstance, every challenge, every situation we may find ourselves in. Paul says much about this in Romans 8:

"I consider our present sufferings are not worth comparing with the glory that will be revealed in us ... in all things God works for the good of those who love him ... If God is for us, who can be against us? ... No, in all these things we are more than conquerors ... I am convinced that ... nothing in all creation will be able to separate us from the love of God that is in Christ Jesus our Lord."

(Romans 8: 18, 28, 31, 37, 38, 29 – but it is well worth studying the whole tremendous chapter!)

The *larger* our view of God, the *smaller* will seem our concerns. That is not spiritual sleight of hand, it is the way we are meant to conduct our lives. It is setting our sights high. Many of our problems stem from the fact that we have far too small a view of God. Too small a vision of him.

Sometimes you will hear someone say: "Oh I wish I had your faith." Actually it is not great faith which counts. It is faith in a great God which matters in the end. If we are willing, God will help us sort out the issues in our lives, and the issues under the surface. He can do it, if we'll let him. He is totally sufficient, and wants us to trust him. And we'll be able to trust much better if we face the truth, and see God as he really is.

Where do you Stand?

Real freedom comes from knowing and appropriating the truth about God, as it is found in Jesus. As he is real and he is there, we need to meet him, talk with him, and be prepared for him to change us, if all this is going to turn out to be meaningful for us. So, where do you stand? Long-cherished attitudes are hard to part with. On the other hand, Jesus does bring real liberty when we turn over our lives to him. If in reading this chapter, God has spoken to you in any way, regarding something of importance about yourself, then don't leave it there. Take some moments, before the day is out, to respond to God. Pray about whatever it is that has come up. Expect God to answer. And learn to trust him. Know that you are accepted. Be prepared for him to guide you. Remember you are forgiven. It is real cause to give thanks and praise.

Chapter Seven

KEEPING THE CAR ON THE ROAD – EFFECTIVE SELF-MANAGEMENT

From the cradle upwards we are taught to look after ourselves. At home, at school, right the way into adulthood, we receive varied and comprehensive instruction as to how to preserve our fragile frame from harm and discomfort. From the newspapers, magazines, television, radio, numerous publications of all sorts, we are constantly being offered advice of every shape and size. And all with one purpose. To help us live longer, healthier, happier, wiser lives than hitherto possible. We ought, therefore, to be experts on good self-management. Why aren't we?

Some People Never Learn

It was beginning to have an effect on Mary too. Fancy going upstairs at eleven o'clock on a Saturday night to check through your bank statement! And George knows that when he is tired, he always gets his sums wrong. And that only makes him feel worse.

"You should be doing something relaxing before you go to bed, darling." Mary rather weakly made her thoughts known. She knew it would not make much difference.

One of the big anxieties for Mary has made its appearance only fairly recently. What if something happened to George?

He is driving himself so fast. It is not good for him at his age. And what would we all do if he should die? The fear of losing a partner is a poignant and difficult emotion to deal with. George was not exactly helping matters by his compulsive over-activity.

"I'll be in bed in half an hour, sweetheart," George reassured his wife. "I've not got too much to do. But I must do it tonight. There won't be any time tomorrow."

Mary wasn't sure that she agreed. George had taken to going to the early service at church. Mary thought it was a good measure temporarily to help him put his feet up for the rest of Sunday morning. But after only a week, George was using the spare time on Sunday to rush around everywhere fixing this, fixing that – under the car, on top of the roof. No relaxation at all. It really annoyed Mary one particular week, when, after all this hectic activity, George took himself off on his own to the pub round the corner, drank four pints and then, arriving home late, refused his Sunday lunch because he wasn't hungry!

"I wouldn't mind so much, darling, if you'd just pace yourself a bit more. But your secretary says you're trying to prove yourself the office whizz-kid. At home, you never seem to have time to visit any of our friends or have them come here. Your diary is piled high with work appointments, so when do we ever get a chance to get out together? You always used to say that when the children grew up, we'd have time to do the things we used to do when we were first married . . ."

Mention of the children stung George with guilt. He still felt responsible for Amanda. If only he had been able to spend more time with her when she was younger. "I'll see you in half an hour. Leave the light on."

Mary was still awake, thoughts buzzing through her head, when George reappeared. The bedside clock said one o'clock. George's mental arithmetic was not what it used to be . . . George would need to be up again at half past six. At least, he thought, I won't have to talk to anyone at the eight o'clock Communion!

Every motor car manufacturer proudly announces that its product is built to last. Most of us know that a significant proportion of those we see on the scrap heap simply have not been looked after. Just as a car needs careful handling, regular check-ups and servicing, and respect for its limitations, not pushing it too hard or too fast for long periods, so do human beings. We ought to be experts in looking after ourselves. Strangely, we are not. So keeping the car on the road – good self-management – is essential if we are going to avoid the worst symptoms, particularly of stress, but of anxiety too.

It is important to remember that what happens to us may well affect others as well. One person's stress can have a knock-on effect and produce anxiety in someone else, as we have just seen with George and Mary. Coping with the stress and anxiety of others, especially those close to us, can be quite an exhausting exercise long term. So we have an obligation, not only to ourselves, but also sometimes to other people, to ensure our efforts to look after ourselves are sensible and responsible. We have to learn to be effective self-managers.

Here is a check list for personal care:

1. Physically – watch your diet and exercise.
2. Socially – maintain and develop friendships and time off.
3. Emotionally – keep checking those attitudes.
4. Strategically – pace yourself, and give thought to long-term planning and goals.
5. Spiritually – nourish your relationship with God through prayer/Bible reading/worship/fellowship/service and giving.

Stop at the Check Out!

Stop for an instant, and have a thought about each of these five areas. Before we examine them in any further detail, it will be good if you can review where you feel you are in respect of each of these. In this way, knowing your present performance, you will be in a better position to benefit from the development of the ideas which follow. So stop at the check out now. See what your score is. When you have done some self-assessment, then carry on with what comes next.

Diet and Exercise – Physical Management

Mary thought that George ought if anything to be *losing* weight. It was probably his drinking which caused him to be growing slightly flabby. The pathetic little tales of missed lunchtime snacks, or the single sandwich gulped in a mouthful, only increased her concern that at home George's eating habits were poor indeed. He was getting used to throwing his food down, eating the fats and the stodge, and leaving all the protein and vegetables at the side of his plate. Rarely now did he take any exercise. His life was a cycle of work – travel – exhaustion – sleep – work, and so on.

Sarah, by contrast, has had a happier time recently. The real advantage of living near Peter's parents is that his mother is only too willing to babysit. Sarah and Peter together have joined a squash club locally. It is a terrific break each week, apart from being marvellous exercise. Neither of them was sure who felt more battered after their first game at the new club! They had forgotten they had so many muscles, and every single one felt sore and stretched. It was like riding a horse for the first time. But after a few more games, they were both feeling more toned up. What a help it was.

Sarah had to put her foot down about one thing, however. Peter had developed an enormous appetite following each and every game. Since she had managed to get his weight down on that high fibre diet, it was going to be sensible eating from now on. Sarah was resolute!

What can we learn about physical management – diet and exercise, from George, Sarah and Peter? A keyword here is *discipline*. George is lacking it, Sarah and Peter are increasing in it.

It is essential that we look after our *diet*, what we eat, and our *eating pattern* – the way we eat. When we are under stress or anxious there is a pressure to disrupt healthy eating habits, with consequent effects upon our well-being.

Discipline sounds an uncomfortable word. All it means is to recognise that God has made us to be governed by certain basic physical laws, essential to our physical, mental and spiritual equilibrium. Balanced regular diet forms part of this framework.

It is sometimes said, you are what you eat. Certainly it is true we need a balanced diet if we are not to abuse our bodies. It is also true that healthy eating patterns are equally important to health in this area.

So a regular diet containing a good balance of protein, vitamins, some carbohydrate and adequate roughage is essential: the old formula of fish or meat, vegetables and so on. In our pre-packaged world, it is worth trying to cut out as much processed food as possible. We all need a healthy intake of high fibre foods. Of course, it takes effort – discipline – to ensure you regularly do eat like this. Equally, it takes discipline to ensure you eat both enough, and not too much. Fortunately, in healthy people the appetite usually ensures about the right intake, no more no less within reason. But it only takes a little indiscipline to throw the balance off centre.

Peter had started to eat to compensate. Though things had improved, he was unsettled about his new job. Fortunately, Sarah had seen through that one, before it was too late. Anxiety can send us both ways, as can stress, off our food or on to it in a big way. Discipline ensures regular and wise eating habits. Sometimes it means arguing with yourself, when your battered appetite is telling you something which is plainly not going to do you any good. "Leave it – you're not hungry." "Get some chocolate from the shop – it won't spoil your appetite." "One more piece won't matter – it would be a shame to leave it." It is all lies, isn't it?

Eating patterns are another factor. Regular meals taken at a leisurely pace are an important element in our ongoing well-being. Slouching in a chair, gulping a sandwich for three minutes, then chasing off round the office to find out if the

photocopier is free now, does no one any good. Meal times
provide a change of pace during the day. Ideally, they provide
opportunities to converse in a relaxed way with others. The
relaxed atmosphere aids digestion. You nourish your body,
it feels better, it can serve you more happily for the rest of the
day. You look after it, it will look after you.

Peter had to stop his habit of "snacking" – eating between
meals. George needs to do some work on providing a decent
lunch hour for himself, and getting out of the office for a
stroll. Exercise does not have to be very energetic, but it
should exist.

Exercise is an important part of physical management. It is
not just to keep the joints moving, either, though that is no
bad idea. The benefits to the mind as well as the body of a
walk round the shops at lunchtime, or out in the countryside
or wherever, are enormous. The brain slows down, so does
your pulse rate; physically and mentally you are doing
yourself good. Any kind of exercise, with your mind on the
exercise itself and not on other things, helps your strained
inner self realise there is another world – a world bigger than
your immediate concerns. It is a pleasant and worthwhile
diversion. If you miss it, you miss out. Healthy routine is also
something to which our minds and bodies respond well.
Regular patterns for sleeping and waking, if interrupted,
often cause stress to build up unawares. So loving attention to
routine helps our bodies as well, and should not be neglected.
Are you aware of your need for routines? They form an
important element in our general equilibrium.

In general, looking after your body, through good diet,
regular exercise and sensible routines, is no optional extra.
Our handling of anxiety and stress are much poorer when we
do not. To do it means simply one word: DISCIPLINE.

Friends and Recreation – Social Management

One of the most helpful things to come out of joining the
squash club, as far as Peter is concerned, is the new circle of

friends he and Sarah have been able to establish. Sarah, of course, is delighted. She thought when she gave up work she would never make any new friends – ever. It does sometimes seem like that. But all that has changed. And she is more outgoing now as well. Peter is finding the fact of having friends to visit and do things with, is taking his mind off work as well. More than that, it is getting everything more into proportion. It helps your own troubles get back into focus when you see what other people go through. It has been good to lend a helping hand with one or two friends they have made from the club, who have been in trouble recently.

Mary had at last taken the plunge. She had been meaning and wanting to join one of the small groups at the church for a long time. It was not that George was holding her back. He was quite happy for Mary to join a fellowship group on her own. But Mary felt it would have been so much nicer if George had joined too. However, the meetings over the last six months had been such a pleasure, such warm people, so supportive. The usual pattern was coffee and cake, then a Bible study. Then some sharing of issues of personal concern, with some prayer following, either silently or out loud – you could do it either way depending on how you felt. Then more coffee to finish. The new Christian friends had been a real joy, and a great support. Mary had felt able, privately, with two woman friends in the group, to talk about her predicament with George. Their love and understanding removed weighty burdens from Mary's shoulders. They were so understanding. It was simply wonderful when they prayed for George – and also to know they would go on praying.

Everybody needs friends. And it is unwise to neglect them. Friends are those people we can relax with. The people with whom we can be ourselves. The ones who accept us.

Relationships like this don't just grow on apple trees. We have to be prepared to work at them. That means time. And some of us haven't much of that to spare. It depends really on priorities. The Bible underlines it for us as a fact of our creation. God said to Adam: "It is not good for man to be alone." And although occasional solitude is welcome, even necessary – after all Jesus would often withdraw from the crowds – nonetheless we must not forget we are social creatures. We are made to be that way. We all *need* friends.

Given that fact of our creation, it is relatively easy to see why when we neglect these kinds of relationships we suffer. Some sociologists point to the fact that it is difficult to maintain and sustain more than twelve close friendships in any circle. Certainly Jesus had twelve disciples, and within that group there were some closer than others. If Jesus is our model, we can see that the one thing he seemed to avoid was superficiality.

He spent time with people, and he chose a manageable number with whom to spend particular time, developing and growing in relationship and friendship.

The point then is obvious. We also need to make time for people, for friends. Normally when you invest care and interest in others, they respond with theirs. Superficiality kills relationships. It says: "I'm not interested in you as a person." And we all need and long to be treated as people. We have feelings, they need to be listened to; thoughts and ideas, they need to be respected and understood. We have inner and practical needs, these require kind, caring action. When we are able to give and take in this way, we are more whole people.

Friends and recreation in some ways go hand in hand. Sarah and Peter met their friends at the squash club. Mary at the fellowship group. Doing things together is an important part of building friendships. Just as the more time you spend in one another's company, the greater the potential for growth in the relationship.

Recreation implies relaxation. God has designed it so that we have one day in seven given entirely to activities other than work. This Sabbath principle we violate at our peril. After all the Creator knows best. And do not forget that holidays are important too. It is also important for a healthy mind to have a general balance of activities. Most people have hobbies, and it is counter productive to neglect them. Of course, sometimes work needs to be brought home, but reading company reports in bed at night is a recipe for bad sleep and ulcers!

We have to learn to pace ourselves, and help the equilibrium of our lives by varying the input too. Friendships, relaxing, diverting activities, are the stuff of which the settled mind is made. Stress and anxiety do not flourish in an environment so well organised and cared for as this.

Attitudes and Outlook – Emotional Management

The two friends of Mary's own age had been very supportive. It was so good to know that Mary could phone them up at any time, if she became desperate, or something happened. But it had been much better recently. Not that George had changed. Would that he might! Though in a sense Mary's more relaxed ways were beginning to affect George positively, just as his tense attitude to everything had been undermining Mary. However, she had caught herself getting into the fussing syndrome again recently. "George is going to hurt himself. We'll never manage. Why doesn't God stop him? I'm not going to be able to cope." It had been past history as far as Mary was concerned. She had stopped taking notice of those old voices, thinking they had gone for good. It was a surprise when they reappeared.

It is odd how you sometimes want to worry and hang on to your anxieties. They may be painful, but in a perverse way, they are like old friends. Mary struggled too. But she made it. The passage they had been studying last Tuesday had helped. "If anyone is in Christ, he is a new creation; the old has gone, the new has come!" (2 Cor. 5:17). The old way of life has come to an end, thought Mary. If God has given me a new life and his Holy Spirit, how silly to let myself slip back into those old ways again.

Sarah knew that she was loved. There was such tangible

evidence of that: Peter's care, his parents' interest in her as a person; Daniel's loving attitude to his mum. And now so many new friends. What a new experience it was for Sarah.

But, above all, it had been learning again about God's own special deep love for her, his complete acceptance of her, which had helped Sarah. It was something she needed to keep on reminding herself about. When they had invited a young policeman and his wife over for supper one evening, Sarah had found herself panicking. "Maybe they'll think I'm boring. What if the supper doesn't turn out right ... God loves me just as I am. I've got all these other friends. Of course it will turn out OK."

Old attitudes die hard. So if we have struggled to master an outlook on life or some area of experience which has been troublesome for us, the chances are it will try to make an unwelcome appearance again from time to time. George's perfectionism was like that. He had tried to work at it. Did quite well too, for several months. Then, when things were going a little less well in terms of other people's management decisions, he found himself getting noticeably uncomfortable.

Until, that is, he realised it was his perfectionist trait coming out again. After all it didn't really matter, did it, if everything wasn't absolutely perfect? He would just have to learn to live with imperfect people in an imperfect world! And it worked.

So a regular check-up on our attitudes is good and useful. A regular question to ask ourselves is, what has been my dominant attitude over the last month? Have I been negative, positive, fearful, joyful or whatever – and why? Is my attitude justified by the events and the facts? A check-up on general attitudes is as important as to the particular attitudes we embody. It is easy to slip into an unrealistic attitude, and hardly be aware we have done so. Until, at least, stress and anxiety symptoms begin to catch up with us. They love something to latch on to. So be warned.

Planning and Pacing – Strategic Management

George was sitting in a traffic jam. For some people nothing is such a nail-biting experience. Driving anyway these days is stressful enough. George had taken to driving the car up to London because the trains had become too much for any civilised man to bear. For a while the idea had been working fine. He had been getting up earlier than usual to leave before the other traffic found its way on to the motorway. And he would set out home an hour after everyone else, to ensure a reasonably trouble-free ride home. But, as Mary had pointed out, he was getting even less rest than usual. It was the old law of diminishing returns. So today he had decided to drive in and drive back along with the masses . . . it was awful!

It was then it came to him. George didn't know why the idea hadn't clicked before. Why bother with all this needless stress of travelling to and fro to the city every day? When he was starting out and getting established, that was different. But now, with his experience and qualifications he could surely get a job locally. The doctor had said there was nothing wrong with him. But the headaches and indigestion were beginning to get through to George. Maybe he did need to make things easier for himself.

Planning and pacing are elementary, yet so many of us let our lives just happen. Then we strenuously try to fit in with the sometimes hectic or inconvenient shape the pattern of our lives has evolved into. Yet we ourselves have much more ability to control the pattern of our existence than that.

Work quite evidently takes up much of our waking time. George was in a fortunate position to be able to think about changing his job to make life easier for him. But the really important step forward was that he had begun to think about pacing himself.

Pacing yourself is when you introduce a variation of pace into your life. Periods of high activity, punctuated by moments of relaxation, slower movement and so on. Not taking on more than you can manage. Planning strategically. George is the kind of person who normally charges at everything. People like that have to be all the more careful to vary the rhythm a bit.

In the same way, those whose anxiety turns them towards sluggishness equally can learn a thing or two. When Peter was looking for a job and feeling altogether down about things, he tended to let life pass him by. Sarah's suggestion of filling his free time purposefully, was such a useful way of giving him direction and structure to all the time he had on his hands. Not only did the woodwork class improve his skill with a chisel, there were some very handy pieces of Peter's expertise finding their way on to the kitchen wall!

How clearly do you see the overall picture of how your life works out? A diary is very helpful in this respect. A diary is not so much designed to fill up your time, as to organise your time. If you are a busy person, go through your diary carefully even a year ahead and book in some of your priorities. Space them out, so they happen in manageable chunks. Times to visit family and friends, time for outings of various sorts. Time to achieve certain activities which are important to you. Learn to look ahead regularly in the diary. A year, six months, three months, one month. Budget for what will be coming up. And do not take on any more than you can sensibly manage. Of course, you can over-organise yourself (and other people!). If you tend to be like this, try to leave more room for flexibility and spontaneity. Only some kinds of activities take well to a great deal of forward planning. But planning there should be.

The same applies if you are not so busy. Use the diary to help you plan ahead effectively. If you see there might be a lonely period coming up, then prepare for it. The more time you give yourself to organise yourself, the more likely things are to happen to your satisfaction. The real failure is to be crashing into situations and events, simply because you didn't give them enough preparatory thought. You are the one who complains. You are the loser. And you are the one who can do something about it.

An Exercise

Draw on a piece of paper a picture of how you see the pace of your life. Try and show how fast or slowly you feel you are going most of the time, and the relationship between the two. The image can be abstract or realistic. Then ask yourself how you could improve the pacing of your life, both in the short term, and then long-term goals. Do not be afraid to do some realistic planning. Now draw a picture of how you would like your life to be. After you have done that, pray about your findings, and how you would like your life to be. Have the courage to put what you have learnt into practice. Do it now or you may forget.

Praying and Serving – Spiritual Management

Sarah and Peter had started by taking Daniel to the family service. In fact he spent most of the time in the creche. But it was just the right atmosphere for young families. And there was some real teaching. The curate gave a talk for the children, then after they had gone off for their activities, he continued the same theme with the adults. But this time everyone opened their Bibles and studied the passage together.

Since joining the church, Peter has joined a training course to lead a home Bible study group. Sarah is helping with the young wives group. More than that, they have both started to read the Bible at home and to have times of prayer on their own, and also occasionally together too. They find the constant interaction of personal prayer and Bible study very helpful. The worship on Sundays, fellowship with loving Christians, some of whom also play squash, and being involved and contributing their own abilities to the church is all very rewarding. They said it to each other the other day. They both feel so much better.

When George succeeded in getting a position with a local firm of accountants, Mary regarded it as a real answer to prayer. Of course it was long ago that she gave up the idea that

God gives you simply everything you ask for. But she does know he gives you what you need. His wisdom is most reliable on these things. George was impressed too. After all, Mary had said she and her friends had been praying about the idea – six months before George had even thought of it!

Our spiritual lives are just as important, to say the least, as any other aspect of personal management. God has made us to know him. And he has made the church to be the body of Christ, a community of believing people with one purpose and goal in mind: to strengthen each other through friendship, teaching, prayer and worship – and to share the message about Jesus with the outside world. Because we have been made by God to find our ultimate strength from him, through these means, to neglect them inhibits us, and, at the worst, actually harms our progress into full maturity. Dealing with stress and anxiety means catching up with the development of our spiritual lives too.

The Place of Prayer

Prayer is communication with God, sometimes talking, sometimes not talking. But the most important fact to remember when you are praying, is God is your Father, your deeply loving, understanding, tender, Heavenly Father. It would be a good idea to look up in the Bible what Jesus teaches on this great truth about prayer to the father in Luke 11: 1-13. He underlines what is a new truth for us when we become Christians, that God now treats us as his own family, his own children, now that we have received the forgiveness of Jesus, and committed our lives to him. That, by the way, is why all prayer is through Jesus. We often end a prayer "through Jesus Christ our Lord" or "In Jesus' Name" and that is the reason why. Jesus makes access to God possible in the first place.

So, when we pray, this is the truth to remember: because God is our Father, in that supreme sense, he knows our deepest longings. He understands. He is able to meet our needs. He is completely wise, so his decision will be the best one. We can pray and leave the outcome to him. It is an attitude of faith. It needs working at, but it is meant to be the source of all our strength.

A regular time for reading the Bible and praying is essential. There are many kinds of Bible study notes available at different levels, which make the study of the Bible both a pleasure and intelligible. Reading the Bible is, in a sense, God's way of speaking back to us, and therefore important to be taken in conjunction with prayer.

The real point is that we can bring all our concerns, fears, anxieties and pressures to God. We can tell him about all these things. When we get into the habit of trusting God with the whole of our lives, which we will if we start praying regularly, then we will have the joy of seeing our lives unfolding under the sure management of his guiding hand. That is why we have to learn to trust God. Ask him to help you in this. After all, he understands you and the special way you have been made. Always be honest with God. Tell him how you feel. He will always be honest with you.

How long should I pray?

Practically, it is always best to be realistic about prayer times. Do not necessarily try praying all night for your first session! Try as little as seven minutes in a quiet place alone with God to begin with. Be comfortable. You can sit or kneel, whatever is best for you. Be natural, and speak to God in normal language, and ask him to help you get to know him better. You will no doubt need more time as you develop in prayer. There are no rules – just a whole new world to explore. These different elements to do with prayer may help.

Do give God praise for something you have learnt about him, perhaps his justice or kindness, or forgiveness, or something else you have learnt from your Bible reading.

Then, don't forget to confess your sins. As a Christian you are completely forgiven in an overall sense, but it is a matter of clearing the decks, keeping the lines of communication open. None of us will be thrown out of God's family, now we are Christians. But we can do things to spoil relationships "at home" and we need to remember to say sorry.

Then, it is valuable to look back over the past day or week or even longer, and thank God for his kindness to you. Learn to see his hand in your life, and acknowledge this in thanksgiving.

Then, just as important is intercession. That means not to be afraid of asking God to help on behalf of other people or things or situations. The sky is the limit – international politics as well as your own particular concerns. But you will find the opportunity to bring your personal needs to God regularly in this way will be a tremendous help to your stress or anxiety. Of course, it is meant to be like this. God has designed it to be this way. But do not make the mistake of leaving out the other elements of prayer, and going straight to your own concerns – without thought for praise, confession and thanksgiving. Jesus emphasises in that passage on prayer in Luke 11, that these other ways of praying are just as essential. They complete the picture, and keep everything in balance.

Charles Spurgeon, the great Victorian Baptist preacher, used to say, when he went down on his knees, he prayed as though it all depended on God. And when he got up again he acted as though it all depended on him. There is a balance, of course – trusting God's overall power and control, and then co-operating with him and playing our part too. Many of the problems with stress and anxiety stem from the mind set "it all depends on me." If we can crack that one, by a calm dependence on God, we shall make a great deal of progress. Some of us need to repent of our lack of faith, our unreal and unbalanced sense of self-dependence. Others of us need to take steps forward in discovering the richness of knowing God, and his loving concern and will for our lives. It is prayer which enables us to do this. And the easiest way to learn about it is to do it.

The Place of Worship

As people we are both private and public citizens. So as

Christians we have a personal spiritual life, but also a more public or social role in the family of the church. Other Christians are there to help and strengthen us, as well as benefit from our help too. The church (the people not the building) is there to provide opportunities for worship and service which are important for our sense of wholeness as well.

It is true that worship can sometimes be a real turn-off if conducted thoughtlessly. Thankfully most areas have a live church where people can usually feel at home spiritually. Though in general it is best to support your local church, unless you really cannot identify with what is going on there. One fact to remember about worship is that it is not provided to entertain us, but to please God. So to prepare ourselves and be in the frame of mind to *give* our worship is vital if the whole thing is not to turn out an exercise of simply going through the motions. Again, since the meaning of corporate worship is to do it together, it is valuable to get to know and love the Christians you are worshipping with. Since, that is, you are expressing together your love for God.

That is why fellowship, the getting to know and appreciation of other Christians is an important element here. It is again all to do with the way God has made us. We are different from the animals in these respects – we are made to worship God, and enjoy rich relationships with one another. Neglect this design element to our lives and we impoverish ourselves. Again, in worship we experience the greatness and wonder of God, in a way which nothing else can communicate – precisely because it is God communicating back to us. His revelation of himself in the Bible gives us the framework by which to interpret our experience. The meeting with him in worship itself helps make that experience authentic and real. And the larger our vision of God, the more likely we are to want to trust him with those needs close to our hearts. A practical part of worship is our giving. The pocket is usually the last part of us to get converted. But when we learn to give and trust God with our finances, the freedom God brings to us is very considerable indeed. So strengthen yourself through worship in all its factors, and you will be stronger for life itself.

The Place of Service

Most people find that when they contribute something they really feel they belong. And belonging is an important aspect of being part of the church. Somebody once said the church is like a bank, you tend to get out of it what you put into it. The point being made is basically to do with using your abilities and gifts in the church, the idea of helping, or, to use the more usual expression, the idea of Christian service.

Everyone has been given gifts and abilities by God. Paul speaks about this in 1 Corinthians 12:12-31. He makes the point that the church is like a body. It is made up of many parts whilst still retaining its essential unity. And each element of the body has a part to play. The foot does not have to feel hard done by, because it is not an eye!

Nor does the toe need to feel bad because it is not a nose! Each element has a part to play. And the same applies to us. Each of us is unique. We all have something to offer. And we are meant to offer our gifts in service to Christ within the church. You can serve Christ outside the church as well, but the idea here is that everyone has something to offer within the church especially.

What are the things you might be able to help with in your church? Have you ever talked to anyone about your Christian service? Maybe you could get some training for something like leading a Bible study group. But you don't need training to help with the coffee or flower rota. And when those gifts are offered as service to Christ himself, they are just as important as anything else. Everyone is meant to be involved. There is no such thing as a passive Christian in the Biblical sense. So do go and sign up!

Christian service has its spin-offs too. People who serve are people who grow – personally and spiritually. If you are serving Christ, you are centring more on him, and less on yourself, which is important for progress in maturity. You may have no job, or a job that honestly is boring in the outside world. Much fulfilment can come from serving Christ in the church even in small ways. If you serve him from your heart, you will know you are doing something purposeful with your time.

A truly serving church is an attractive vehicle for evangelism. We want to share the good news about Jesus with others. We need to be able to show people that, put at its crudest, the message works! And the sharing of your faith, through patient witness – simply getting on with it, others knowing you are a Christian – provides opportunities to explain about Jesus in your own way when there is an opening.

All this is part and parcel of being a rounded Christian. Such activities, since they are plainly God's will for us, should form the backdrop to all of our lives. A backdrop where the experience of stress and anxiety can in consequence be much better managed simply because we are beginning now to live as God intends us to.

Check Up Regularly

We need to check up regularly to see how our self-management is progressing: the physical; the social; the emotional; the strategic; the spiritual.

Do take these five areas for thoughtful action seriously. Anxiety and stress are like weeds – they need to be dealt with as soon as they arise. Regular maintenance is better than a major overhaul. It is much less traumatic in the end. If we neglect our regular maintenance of effective self-management, we have only ourselves to blame, when life starts getting rough for us. So begin today. Start putting something right now. Don't try and do it all in one go. Little and often is the best advice.

Chapter Eight
WHEN HELP IS NEEDED

There are times in all our lives when the sheer weight of the pressures or concerns we are facing robs us of our confidence that we can overcome or even simply cope with the problems which are before us. Many of us are strangely reticent about seeking help at such times. We would rather suffer in silence than admit to someone else we have come to the end of our resources. Others of us are just the opposite. We throw up our hands in horror at the slightest warning sign, and hotfoot it to the nearest helping professional, whether he be doctor, clergyman, counsellor or whatever. Of course there is a balance between the extremes. There is much we can do to help ourselves, using the resources we already have – in spiritual terms, and within ourselves and from our own circle. But we should never be ashamed of admitting our limitations and needs, and of seeking help when appropriate, especially from those specifically trained and gifted to be of assistance in these areas. So how do you assess when help is needed, and who do you turn to when the need demands it?

Talking it Over

One of the great advantages we all have is the ready-made support of our own circle of friends and family. As we develop in our relationships with friends in particular, all of which is part of effective self-management, we are drawn in to a more intimate sharing of our lives, where we are known, understood and cared for – where the sharing of deep concerns is a natural and unforced possibility. It is true, not everyone has the opportunity for friendships of this sort, but with time and application it is certainly possible to develop in this way.

Those who are married are most likely to develop such a relationship of understanding with their husband or wife. At least that is the ideal. But of course many married people, as well as those who are single, derive enormous benefit from friendships built up with love and devotion carefully over the years. They used to say "a problem shared is a problem halved", and there is much truth in that. In such situations two forces come to bear upon the issue under discussion. First, the venting of the emotion itself related to the issue. "It is good to have got that off my chest." Or, "You've helped me so much, simply by listening." This universal experience reminds us that the simple sharing of a personal concern in an accepting, listening environment, helps release much of the pent-up emotion, which would otherwise press in upon us and make us feel uncomfortable. Secondly, the value of another mind, objectively assessing the situation and weighing the facts, is also both clarifying and supportive in seeking a way forward. Taken together, the idea of simply chatting things over regularly with friends, family or spouses is seen to be highly creative. There is immense value in establishing this normal pattern, of release of emotion and situation assessment, as a regular part of our everyday lives. In consequence this provides a preventative measure in the approach to effective stress and anxiety management. The warning is, those who fail to do this run up considerable risks, and often run into trouble too.

Getting Uptight

The contrast between George and Mary was growing more acute by the week. Mary was finding her new friends in the fellowship group a great strength, especially Evelyn and Elizabeth – the two women of about her own age who had taken Mary under their wing and really taken the trouble to get to know her and care for her. The group, of course, had invited George endless times to come along to their meetings and social occasions, not pressurising him, but always being sure he knew there was an open invitation at any time.

Yet there had been no response. George refused to come to the supper party they organised just recently. It was a little to Mary's discomfort, as George was now working locally and no longer had the excuse of arriving home late in the evenings. The one lunch party he had deigned to attend, one Sunday after morning service, George had parked himself in a corner with one of the administrative assistants from his office who also happened to go to that church, and talked shop for an hour – refusing to be introduced to anyone else – and then he insisted on taking Mary home on the dot of two o'clock! George was becoming socially very resistant.

The contrast between them was growing all the more obvious. Mary was becoming so much more relaxed and open. Even Ben and Amanda noticed it. Yet George was growing more and more tight-lipped by the week.

"Why doesn't Dad see any of his friends any more?" Ben asked his sister, that same Sunday afternoon of the lunch party.

"I don't know," Amanda answered. "He never seems to have time to talk to anyone these days. He doesn't even really talk to Mum either. I think he resents her going to that group at church. Stupid if you think about it, because he could go too. But he doesn't talk to us or anybody." Amanda was actually quite concerned about her father.

"Mum says the reason Dad gets up so early to work at his desk before he goes in the morning is that he is sleeping so badly at the moment," Ben commented. "I don't know why he should be so uptight all the time. He practically bit my head off when I asked for a lift across town last night. He could have just said it wasn't possible. Do you think he is finding this new job less good then he imagined?"

Amanda was quick in reply. "The only thing I think is that he is cutting himself off from everyone. And if something is going wrong, we are likely to see the steam coming out of his ears pretty soon. Because if he doesn't talk about it, there's no other way of getting it out of his system. It wouldn't surprise me if he exploded one day ..."

A Mind at Ease

After all, what are friends for? That was Penny's thought as she pondered mentioning to Jane something serious which had been on her mind. It would be rather a reversal of roles, as Penny had been the listening ear to Jane, especially recently as Jane had come to Christ, and Penny had been helping her get established.

It is always good to talk over a hamburger. Penny explained to Jane her worries about boyfriends ... or the lack of them.

"The thing is, Jane, I am wondering whether there is something wrong with me. I'm getting on now. I mean, I am twenty-three, and I've never had a steady boyfriend! And I do want to get married. And I know all these things are in the Lord's hands, and I want to be patient. But it is difficult, isn't it?"

Penny is a mature girl, but clearly she feels all this very deeply. She is hardly on the shelf, by any manner of means, but she is genuinely unsettled. And the way she feels is the most important factor at the moment.

Jane had learnt from Penny herself that often it is simply best to listen, and show you understand, so she held herself back from offering advice at this stage.

After a while Penny stopped and said: "You're marvellous, Jane, you really understand. I feel so much better now. And I know exactly what to do. I've been trying too hard. I must relax about it, and accept what happens. Thank you so much for helping me." Penny smiled warmly at Jane. "Shall we get some more chips?"

Jane thought that sounded a good idea. She realised she had not said a word for the last twenty minutes. Who would have thought that being prepared to shut up and listen could be such a help?

Talking about it really does help. This kind of talking is like housework. Keeping the house clean and tidy is so much easier if you do a regular tidy-up and dust-around. Leave it untouched for a few months until it becomes a regular tip, and it can become a major operation to ever get things straight again. So it is with talking it over. The self-sufficiency outlook is a myth in some senses. We all need others. It is dangerous to cut ourselves off from other people's care and understanding. But if we regularly discuss the things which are issues for us, not of course purely for the sound of our own voice, but being sensitive to others as we do so, then we shall avoid many major difficulties later on, just as Penny did with Jane. George is different. He is determined to be "self-sufficient". No one is going to know about his inadequacies. And look where it is getting him.

That is not to say there is nothing we can do to help ourselves. Here is the balance. We can equally veer to the other position and never do anything to help ourselves win through. So what can we do to help out as far as our own life is concerned?

Help Yourself

Jane has learnt a great deal about herself in these early months of becoming a Christian. She has understood so much more clearly some of her basic needs, as well as some of her weaknesses and habits of mind and life.

"Maybe it is because I am not afraid to face myself any more," Jane commented to Penny as they were walking back to Penny's room. She was thinking out loud.

"It is marvellous really. Now I know I am accepted by God, and forgiven for all my numerous sins, I can honestly see myself through different eyes."

"Yes, I found that too," added Penny, "when I became a Christian. And the learning process never ends really."

"You'd think I'd be more appalled at myself now, because I realise how bad in God's eyes my life has been. I'd never have dreamt I was a sinner six months ago. In fact if you'd told me, I would have laughed in your face."

"I think you did once, Jane, during the college mission in our first year, when we chatted together after that meeting in the arts centre bar."

"I'd forgotten that," giggled Jane. "You're right about the learning process. I feel now, yes, I realise my weaknesses, but I also recognise that I'm forgiven. And that gives me the freedom to accept the fact that change is necessary. And what's more, I've the impetus to get on and do something about it. Do you get what I mean?"

Penny knew exactly. And they continued to talk about how a deeper knowledge of your true self, through Christ, gives you valuable insight into the area where changes need to be made. It is true, the learning process never ends.

There is so much we can do to help ourselves. And we also have an obligation to do so. Anxiety and stress are greatly helped when we do not shrink from doing the hard and sometimes painful work on our attitudes and behaviour that this kind of help implies.

This emphasis appears in several places in the New Testament. Consider these words of the Apostle Paul, as he sums up the message of his Epistle to the Romans: "And so, dear brothers, I plead with you to give your bodies to God. Let them be a living sacrifice, holy – the kind he can accept . . . Don't copy the behaviour and customs of this world, but be a new and different person with a fresh newness in all you do and think." Romans 12: 1–2 (The Living Bible)

At the heart of these words, is this idea of change – and becoming what God wants us to be – "A new and different person". The "fresh newness" in all we do and think involves two stages. First being prepared to offer our lives to God for his glory. You will notice the word "holy" there. It means being "set apart" or "different". So secondly, God wants us to be tangibly different, and that is seen in the refusal to copy the "behaviour and customs of this world."

How does that work out in practice?

A very basic approach in helping in any situation of anxiety or stress is to ask myself: am I prepared to let this particular situation be given to God for his glory? Not, you note, just treating God like a genie in a lamp and saying: "Here, you sort it out!" But saying to God: "Here is the situation, I'll make room for you to be involved right at the centre, so the glory will come to you."

And there is one further step, it is the necessary consequence. That is to overhaul both attitudes and behaviour rigorously, so that they are not secondhand versions of the perhaps accepted, but non-Christian, values of the society around. It is so easy to unquestioningly accept the values and outlook of those around us, without ever asking whether this is appropriate for Christians at all.

Values do need to be overhauled, changes do need to be made. Most counsellors encounter resistance at this very point. Here is a situation where a man of thirty arrives, complaining of anxiety concerning his girlfriend who is threatening to leave him. The fact that the fellow is married, and has been sleeping with this girl who is not yet in her twenties, provides plenty of complications. He has come for help with his anxiety. If he is a Christian, and it is not unknown, sadly, for Christians to get themselves in these tangles, the real way forward is to end the sinful behaviour and be reconciled with his wife. That removes the major anxiety factors, but more important it is putting God first. And God does not let us down when we do that. In fact it is the way forward for anyone, but clearly the big question is, who makes the rules? Where do you derive your values from?

Say you are a person who works best at a hundred miles an hour. You perhaps have a tendency to be touchy when tired, or perhaps an inferiority complex, which causes you to be unpleasantly assertive. The realistic knowledge of yourself in these areas, a willingness to face the real you and be prepared to change, is vital if you are going to grow and mature and make progress. But that, honestly, is the biggest issue. Are you prepared to change? Or are you like the young man who wanted to get rid of his anxiety, but wasn't prepared to alter his sinful behaviour and end his adultery. You can't have it both ways. So when help is needed, unless we are prepared to help ourselves, all the help in the world from other people will not finally be of any lasting value. This is serious. Do ask yourself: am I prepared to change? Be courageous. Those who put God first in this way are never disappointed. But those who in the final analysis are not prepared to change – they are always frustrated, and sometimes the outcome is even worse.

When you get Stuck – Who to Turn to

There is no shame in seeking help. Just as it is the most natural thing to speak with family and friends – chatting over a problem or issue – so when you come to the limits of that kind of help, the professionals have invaluable services to offer. It is a matter of the treatment fitting the injury. You wouldn't dream of not sticking a plaster on a cut finger if needed. So why not a specialised counsellor when a particularly acute case of anxiety and stress equally requires special treatment?

That said, there is a hurdle we need to get over in seeking special help. It is to do mainly with our pride, in that we all feel, understandably, that baring our soul to a professional can sometimes invoke fear or shame within us. There are worries about confidentiality or not being taken seriously, concern that either I am making a mountain out of a mole hill or I may be going mad. The fact is, seeing someone about the concern means the issue has to be faced. Something has to be done about it. And sometimes, though we would like relief from the more unpleasant feelings associated with our problems, we have grown used to the general situation, and we are not so sure we want it to change. So that is a hurdle we simply have to overcome. If you want it finally sorted out, the only way is to seek help. It is the most sensible thing to do.

It Feels Like Defeat

Unbeknown to Mary, George had gone off to the doctor. It was the same GP he had seen some months back, when he was suffering from those headaches. He had not been back since then, but life had become so intolerable for him, he had to talk to someone. And, though it felt like defeat, the doctor had been so kindly when he saw him last time, George hoped it might be all right.

"I seem not to be able to stop grinding my teeth together," George stammered out, as he began his consultation. "I hate doing it, but I can't stop it. And I'm getting terrible indigestion too. But, what is worse, I feel as though I'm going to explode inside."

The doctor listened quietly as George struggled to say what was on his mind.

"You see, I've always felt that I had to fill every moment of my day with purposeful activity. It was all right when I was young, I could afford to rush around, and take on more than most people. But now it is different. I've recently taken an easier job locally to reduce my load, but I've filled up the spare time with other things. It's not sensible, I know. But I don't seem to be able to stop myself. Add to that some problems with Amanda. And even though Mary is wonderful, really marvellous, I don't think I can cope any more. I feel I'm going to explode. My head is tight. I feel terribly on edge. All I want to do is cry."

As he said it George could not believe it was really him talking. And yet here he was, a man of his age, choking back the tears. What was happening to him?

"Crying does help," the doctor said.

So out it came. And with it a full, frank explanation of all the problems, hang-ups and anxieties George had been living with for so many months, and in some ways, years.

It was quite a release. At last, George was on the road to getting himself straightened out.

When we get stuck, the most sensible thing we can do is talk to someone who will really understand. Understand at two levels. At the level of our feelings, they will be able to identify with us, giving us the impression of acceptance. This is deeply reassuring, for when we are feeling vulnerable the last thing we want is not to be taken seriously, to be laughed at, or worse, be rejected out of hand. Identification then is paramount.

Then our difficulties need to be properly understood. The helping professional always asks himself the question: what is going on here? He tries to get as full a picture as possible, to help the sufferer unravel the tangles. We can't expect these people to make decisions for us. But we can expect them to help clarify a situation, so that we are better equipped to make decisions for ourselves, or take other appropriate action.

However, we have to help them to help us. We must be prepared to tell the professional helper the whole story, even the bits that embarrass us. After all, these people have talked to so many about their lives, they have learnt these two lessons. First, that there is nothing new under the sun. They have heard it all before. That doesn't make them any the less sympathetic, but it is difficult to shock them. The other fact is, they know that beneath the surface everybody, absolutely everybody, has their difficulties and sensitivities. So there is no losing face in telling them the full truth. They are the realistic ones, they know that no one is perfect. But they do know there is opportunity for change. And that is why it is worth talking it all through.

Whom Should I Choose?

There are many different kinds of professional help available. Which is the best one to turn to?

Sometimes we choose individual personalities who we feel will "understand" our problem. Other times the choice factor concerns the specific skill the helping professional has to offer. There is no general best kind of professional help. Each need is different and has to be assessed accordingly.

DOCTORS, especially GPs, are the first port of call for many. General practitioners are experienced in helping with anxiety and stress in particular, as much of their case load comes from these two common problems. There are several advantages of a talk with your GP. One is the assurance of confidentiality. If you are fortunate enough to get to know your doctor over a number of years, he is able to build up a fairly comprehensive picture of you, which is clearly of real value. But though GPs are very willing to help, their time is limited, and sometimes it is not possible to talk at the length or frequency the situation demands – though many GPs do try to give their patients extra time when circumstances permit. Doctors also deal much with medication. Wonderfully valuable though this is in many cases, sometimes the offer of tranquillisers or sleeping pills is at best only a stop-gap measure, and at worst a ducking out of the responsibility to get to the root of the problem. Many times such medication is just what is needed. It is difficult not to believe, however, that sometimes such medication is offered as a substitute for talking things through. And sometimes the fault lies with the patient, who would prefer to be anaesthetised to the pain of the situation, rather than face the issues and sort it out that way. Help your GP to help you. They are skilled and caring people. They want to help you if they can.

Doctors do vary like anyone else in their counselling skills. It is always possible to be referred for further specialised help if necessary. We shall look in the next section at when specific medical help is required, as it sometimes is. But remember you are being a little unfair if you are expecting your doctor to be able to give you something he is neither trained nor appointed to do. If your situation touches on values, your inner world, spiritual life and so on, you may well need a different kind of counsellor.

CLERGYMEN AND MINISTERS OF RELIGION. Again it is a case of choosing your man (or woman). Many clergy these days have specialist training in pastoral counselling, and can offer a wide range of skills particularly applicable to Christians. Again a clergyman is likely to have several advantages. He may well know you in a wide variety of settings, in the church, the community and so on – so he has a broad picture, before he begins, of you as a person. He will help you draw close to God and his resources for change. And you can be sure he will pray for you regularly when any concern of yours is particularly pressing. You may find your clergyman or minister is more accessible than your doctor. Certainly, like any of the other counselling specialists, he will be able to give adequate time to uninterrupted talking through of your needs. He will inevitably be a person of broad experience of life and human nature. Just because he wears a clerical collar, does not mean he is easily shocked, far from it. So do not be afraid of telling him the whole truth. We are all afraid of losing face. But the clergy above all are in the forgiveness business. They know that God forgives sinners, and they want you to know it too. It is the most healing truth they have to offer. There are also an increasing number of women involved today in full-time ministry in the church. Their presence has enriched enormously the resources of compassionate understanding and skill that the church can offer through its professional, pastoral and counselling ministry.

COUNSELLORS of one type or another offer another avenue of help. Some specialise in marriage counselling, family therapy or other specific areas. Others offer more general help in the counselling field. In several larger cities Christians are in the forefront of developing counselling agencies of this sort.

London's Care and Counsel is run entirely by Christians, professionally skilled and qualified, and offers help with all kinds of emotional and personal problems, within a distinctively Christian framework. Local libraries usually contain a list of most of the counselling agencies in a community. It is best, like many things, to ask around and get some recommendations. Doctors and clergy can help with this information too.

SOCIAL WORKERS, TEACHERS, YOUTH WORKERS and several others also, all have skills in this area. The important issue is to choose someone you think will deliver the goods, someone who will have the appropriate tools to respond to your needs, and someone whom you can talk to. So consider what you think is your specific need. Ask around as to who is good in that area.

Should I Only See a Christian Counsellor?

Christians often ask this question, and it is good to consider it. We are all made in the image of God, irrespective of whether we are committed to Christ or not. So Christians don't have the monopoly on skills and insight – far from it. A Christian counsellor will understand you as a Christian, and will be particularly helpful if there are definite spiritual dimensions to your needs. Yet a non-Christian counsellor will still respect your Christian convictions.

The main factor is simple: is this person good at what he does? Is he or she sympathetic, insightful? Does he listen well and ask appropriate questions helpfully? So it is a question of whether the need requires Christian help specifically, and who is the best person to go to. Some feel more at ease with a Christian counsellor, though in some cases the fact the counsellor *is* a Christian may not turn out to be relevant at all to the specific situation. Nonetheless, we all need encouragement to approach our problems in a Christian way. A Christian counsellor will obviously help in this direction, providing the other factors are properly covered as well.

Beware of the Witch Doctor Mentality

The person you are going to see is only another *ordinary*

human being, subject to the same strengths and weaknesses as yourself. They are not superhuman, neither can they wave a magic wand over you. Some people are never happy when they come away from the doctor unless they have been given a prescription for a magic potion. Sometimes a prescription is not necessary. The doctor should know what he is doing. Always you need to do something to help yourself, particularly with anxiety and stress where there are no easy answers on offer. But there are always ways forward – if only we will travel them.

When Anxiety and Stress are Part of an Illness

There are times when the doctor will definitely be the first port of call for anxiety and stress symptoms, when these are clearly part of an illness. There are times also when we need to be aware that prolonged or severe anxiety and stress can have a negative effect on our physical well-being. The best advice in these circumstances is always to ask. Doctors are used to dealing with these questions, and usually they are able to set your mind at rest.

If action is required, then the earlier this happens, the better. If there seems to be any unusual or unfamiliar features you have begun to notice about yourself, then seek help. It comes back to self-management. If you know yourself properly, you will be able to recognise anything unusual or untoward good and early.

The Mumps and Measles of the Soul

It was Charles Lamb, the English essayist, who once described the experience of depression in these graphic terms. Nowadays we understand that depression can be an illness in its own right, rather than simply an attack of the blues. As such, clinical depression is often accompanied by acute anxiety which is extremely distressing to the sufferer. Nothing will relieve it, however "sensible" about things the depressed person tries to be. So sometimes, an unintentional confusion takes place, and the anxiety is taken for the major problem by sufferer and helper alike – when in reality, it is the depression which needs attention. It is a skilled business to make this distinction – specialised help is needed from a doctor specifically trained in this area. But so much can be done to help with depression if we are prepared to seek assistance in this most painful of afflictions.

There are other mental conditions, besides depression, where anxiety or stress are symptoms. Again, in any case of prolonged discomfort, it is best to seek help – if only to have your mind reassured that all is well.

Reacting to Illness

As we grow older all of us find the aches and pains of life discomforting. The loss or deterioration of a faculty such as hearing or sight is both a worrying and a stressful experience. The fear of illness is common in all of us, but especially as we become more elderly. The concern we have for those who are special to us in life increases with age. The idea of a partner or parent becoming terminally ill or dying is especially difficult. When there is the sudden onset of an illness or physical impairment, especially during the time before the diagnosis, there is usually considerable and understandable anxiety. *Resentment* to an illness itself can bring anxiety symptoms which can sometimes be even more damaging in their effect than the original disease. Add to that long-term or painful treatments, or those sadly incapacitating diseases which require procedures such as amputation or the removal of a breast, and it becomes clear that our reactions to illness are a considerable cause of both anxiety and stress. Public information can equally be the source of such concern. Cancer scares, AIDS scares and the like are all examples. Similarly the fear of heart attack or other illnesses can cause considerable anxiety and distress for many.

Contributing to Illness

Prolonged stress or anxiety is said to contribute to a variety of physical conditions, reinforcing the truth that we are mental and physical units, and that stress is the reaction of the mind and body to change. So heart disease, high blood pressure, angina and heart attacks can well be related to the experience of stress and anxiety. Of course, just because you have been a bit tense just recently, does not mean you are necessarily going to keel over right away! But sometimes there is a link. There is no end to the way stress and anxiety can break out physically.

Many abdominal complaints, such as stomach ulcers and irritable bowel syndrome are related in this way. Migraine is thought to be related to stress, as more clearly are headaches and backaches. Skin problems such as psoriasis and eczema, together with acute loss of hair, are all thought to be associated with stress and anxiety factors in some instances.

All this is quite an encouragement for us to take our stress and anxiety seriously, and do something about them. Our bodies cannot take forever the emotional battering we sometimes give ourselves. We should regard such physical signs when they come as indicators of something needing attention. Very often, strange creatures that we are, we can produce physical symptoms looking every bit like a serious disease, for which, after much investigation, nothing organic is found to account for the signs. Our body has this ability to give out a *cri de coeur* to alert us to the fact that something else is wrong.

Symptoms of Illness

Anxiety and stress can be part and parcel of a physical illness in its own right. Several viral illnesses like flu and glandular fever produce both anxiety and acute frustration.

Such difficult conditions as dementia, Parkinson's Disease or senility also raise profound issues, leading to both anxiety and stress for the unfortunate sufferer. Some drugs too have side effects which produce symptoms like anxiety and stress. In all these ways, the golden rule is check with your doctor if you are at all concerned about yourself.

This considerable catalogue of physically and mentally related conditions shows the ongoing relationship between the functions of mind and body. Such conditions are not necessarily at all related in your own particular case. They only go to illustrate the variety of possibilities there are in helping ourselves to better health and fulfilment – if we are prepared to face and do something about the difficulties which affect us. They also help to fill the broader canvas which enables us to see the variety of ways it may be possible to assist in stress and anxiety, the ways in which stress and anxiety themselves may arise, and, if left unchecked, the ways in which stress and anxiety can do us definite harm.

It should be said there are also normal parts of our lives which cause us personal disruption, which are often associated with stress and anxiety.

The Monthly Cycle

Many women find their monthly cycle a cause of considerable discomfort and inconvenience. Pre-menstrual tension often consists of three particular elements: irritability, depression and lethargy. Tension is the commonest of all the symptoms. It can vary from a simple contrariness, to behaviour which is very far indeed from the woman's normal state of mind. For some, PMT can be particularly distressing.

Irritability often begins with a kind of crabbiness, but can develop into an agitated, jittery feeling. Intolerance, impatience, spite, and often bad temper go with it. It is most distressing for the woman involved. Complications set in when this irritability is accompanied by the moodiness characteristic of depression, and the lazy feeling characteristic of lethargy. Fortunately it does not last too long. In recent years doctors have made progress in understanding and helping with the pre-menstrual syndrome. For the sufferer it is good to take appropriate measures as the time of the month comes round.

If possible take extra rest, rearrange your programme so it is not too pressured and therefore stressful. If there is an issue which always crops up at this time and causes distress, see if you can do something to change things. One couple always had a row when the husband's pay cheque came in. It coincided with the wife's monthly period. So – they changed the date the pay cheque arrived. One problem solved! Such basic self-management decisions are simple but very effective. Above all, if you do suffer, do not feel too guilty. In some ways, it is not the real you. Try and explain yourself to those who will understand, even though some do find this embarrassing. People do understand. Try and do as much as you can with real forethought and imagination to see if you can't improve the situation a little yourself. Don't forget, if there is something which causes you anxiety or stress in general, then when your period comes round, if you haven't dealt with the stress or anxiety factors you may find yourself even more vulnerable. Moral? Don't leave it too long before you sort out any personal issue. Keep short accounts with God and yourself.

We might mention that acute or prolonged stress or anxiety can have an effect on the regularity of periods. During the Second World War some women missed their periods altogether for several years due to anxiety for the safety of their husbands. If you are concerned in any way, do talk to someone qualified about it. Much can be done to help, if need be.

The Change of Life

Both men and women experience what is often called the mid-life crisis, as body and mind adapt to change. For men, the experience is mainly psychological, involving the way they see themselves. For women, however, there are important physical changes too.

The menopause is a natural part of a woman's experience and can occur any time between the ages of thirty-nine and fifty-nine. It occurs when the monthly periods cease and its effects are comparable to and as natural as adolescence, to which it is the counterpart. The change brings emotional response as well. For some women there is a definite experience of moodiness, of which anxiety, stress, depression and other emotions may form a part. The psychological dimensions of the change of life may also be experienced as anxiety in some cases. For those who find this time difficult, it is best to talk to your doctor in the first instance. But in general the change of life does not need to be dwelt upon. It is not an illness, but a normal and healthy transition stage in a woman's life. The best way is to accept each new stage in life which God brings, which of course applies to both men and women. This attitude helps us make the most of each opportunity we are given in our lives to live to the full potential the privileges we have been entrusted with. The change may raise many painful issues of identity, but with understanding and support these may be overcome purposefully.

Bereavement and Grief

However, a major change involving the loss of someone dearly loved and valued requires much readjustment. This can be a time when many issues are raised: practical ones, like how to cope in the future; emotional ones, like a deep sense of helplessness and loss. Grief is very tiring, so when our resources are depleted we have much less in reserve to face the stress or anxiety factors which may well emerge. Don't be afraid of being emotional, when it all comes over you in waves, just when you thought you were doing so well. And don't worry if after almost a year you still feel terrible. It does take time. It doesn't take forever. But it takes longer than most people realise. It is the price we pay for love. It wouldn't

have been much of a relationship, if we didn't miss them.
Acceptance here is a very big help.

The Life Cycle

All of our lives involve a whole series of changes from the
cradle to the grave. Any major change in life is a potential area
for stress or anxiety reaction. It is good to have a think about
what are the major changes in life that everyone goes through.
Thinking about it helps us to be aware they are around the
corner, and helps us accept the inevitability of change too,
and also be prepared to welcome rather than resist the new
experience which change brings in its wake.

Helping a Friend

Sometimes we are going to be the ones to offer help,
friendship, understanding and encouragement to someone
else. How can we best assist them?

A basic requirement is to be a good listener. That means
not interrupting, but letting the person say whatever is on
their mind. You pay no higher compliment than listening
carefully and sensitively. On the other hand, it is easy to
discern when you are not being listened to, and it kills any
helping relationship.

Don't try and be a psychiatrist if you are not one. Damage
can be done if you overstep the limit. Far better to chat over a
cup of tea than be too clinical about it. Avoid the temptation
to give advice. "If I were you, I would . . ." Well, you are *you*,
so the thought is irrelevant. The decisions have to be taken by
the person concerned. The proper response to the questions
"What should I do?" is to throw it back: "What do you feel
are the possibilities open to you?" The responsibility of a
friend is to help *clarify* the situation and the options open,
when a decision is called for. Not, in general, to make the
decision or be giving advice.

The ability to enter into the emotional world of the person

who is unhappy and distressed is also valuable. If you try and recall what it felt like when you went through some painful difficulty, and try putting those feelings into words, then consider what did and did not help you in that situation, you will be better equipped in helping effectively.

Questions are important too. Asking questions which elicit the facts of the situation, and questions which draw out the emotions are the most useful. Questions about the emotions can be direct ("How do you feel about that?") or oblique ("That must have been particularly painful"). Questions about feelings are not necessarily intrusive, they show that you care. Above all, a warm accepting attitude is the most beneficial quality we have to offer.

Those who are able to bring an appropriate word from Scripture offer much assistance, provided it is done with a gentle sensitivity. Prayer itself is so supportive. And the knowledge that prayer will continue speaks powerfully both of your love and the love of God. Such care and loving mutual support of one Christian for another, must have been in the mind of the Apostle Paul, when he wrote: "Carry each other's burdens, and in this way you will fufil the law of Christ." Galatians 6:2

Chapter Nine

Postscript:
IS IT POSSIBLE TO CHANGE?

Is change possible? Can we overcome the difficulties of anxiety and stress? The short answer to that is certainly yes – if we are prepared to face the underlying issues which give rise to these experiences, and deal with them accordingly. The biggest problem is a kind of inertia. We get stuck in a rut, and it is more comfortable to stay there than face the required exertion to climb out again. Beware of such temptation. It carries within itself the seeds of its own destruction. Face the issues you must. The exertion is worth it.

Where are they Now?

We have learnt much from Peter and Sarah, George and Mary, and Jane and her friend Penny. Peter and Sarah are much more settled now. Peter is better settled in his job and himself, and Sarah is being more realistic about her fears of rejection. It has not been easy for them at all, quite an uphill climb, in fact, but neither of them is running away from issues now as they used to. Progress has definitely been made. And Daniel is growing into a charming little boy.

So too for George and Mary. They have also made progress, though George seems to stumble from one crisis to another. He opens up just enough to receive help when the going gets particularly rough, only to return to his old ways when he feels better again. And so the cycle repeats itself.

George *has* made progress, but he needs to be more thorough. He could be braver about it for Mary's sake.

Jane is steaming ahead. Becoming a Christian is the best thing that ever happened to her. Now she is a fully fledged journalist, not in Fleet Street, but on the local paper. She is much better now at organising herself and not overdoing things, and much less worried about what other people think about her.

The Power Comes From God

The real lasting power for effective change comes from God. Often the Holy Spirit is hard at work, unseen, in our talking, thinking and praying, as much in our consultations with others, as our prayerful inner conversations with ourselves. But because of the Spirit's presence in our lives, it means that change is possible. It is a power from God. Weak though we be – he is strong. "We have this treasure in jars of clay to show that this all-surpassing power is from God and not from us." 2 Corinthians 4: 7

So change *is* possible. Facing the problems is the beginning of solving them. And you *can* do it. If you have picked up this book because you have found difficulties in your life which have been painful, even crushing at times, then you are not alone. There are countless millions like you. So much can be done to help the experience of anxiety and stress. Do be courageous, face the issues. Believe in a God who cares for you and can strengthen you. And don't be afraid to seek help. With God's power at work, there is no doubt about it, you can overcome. And when you have, the experience of it, however painful, will in the end make you much better equipped to play your part – to help someone else; to help them *face* the issues underlying *their* anxiety and stress.

Ann Warren

FREE TO BE MYSELF

While the world searches for identity, Christians are supposed to have found it. God promises abundant life and freedom in his service, yet many Christians are struggling under burdens of hopelessness and self-doubt. What has gone wrong?

All too often, writes Ann Warren, Christians accept the world's yardstick for how much they matter as human beings. Past hurts and present fears throw up barriers to self-discovery as a Christian loved and valued by God. Drawing from her personal and counselling experience, Ann Warren shows how these blocks can be lifted, opening the way to personal fulfilment and effective witness.

Ann Warren is a pastoral counsellor, and author of several books.

Elizabeth Heike

A QUESTION OF GRIEF

When cancer robbed Madeleine Fisher of her life, few understood the grief of her close companion, Elizabeth Heike. But for Elizabeth, her friend's death was a bereavement of the deepest kind and shook her world to its core.

'Bereavement has to be lived through,' she writes, 'but it can eventually bring us a resurrection: we can grow through it and indeed find peace and a curious kind of joy.'

A Question of Grief will extend a hand to the isolated and lonely, those who are grieving or in pain. It will also bring insight and understanding to people caring for the bereaved.

'A wise and beautiful book.' *Mary Craig*

'A most challenging and helpful contribution to all who grieve, a book of unusual depth.' *Dame Cicely Saunders*

'Elizabeth Heike's book is one of the most moving I have read.' *Gilbert Kirby*

ELIZABETH HEIKE has worked in the External Studies Department of the London Bible College for the last ten years, writing courses for degree students. She is a founder member of the Hard of Hearing Christian Fellowship, and editor of their magazine.